BEST
CASTLES

ENGLAND ✠ SCOTLAND ✠ IRELAND ✠ WALES

OVER 100 CASTLES TO
DISCOVER AND EXPLORE

BEST
CASTLES

ENGLAND ✚ SCOTLAND ✚ IRELAND ✚ WALES

OVER 100 CASTLES TO DISCOVER AND EXPLORE

D&C
David and Charles

PLANTAGENET SOMERSET FRY

A DAVID & CHARLES BOOK
Copyright © David & Charles Limited 2006

David & Charles is an F+W Publications
Inc. company
4700 East Galbraith Road
Cincinnati, OH 45236

First published in the UK in 2006

This book is based on the research undertaken for
Castles, first published in 2005, which in turn was
based on the research undertaken for *Castles of
Britain and Ireland* by Plantagenet Somerset Fry,
last paperback edition published 2001.

A catalogue record for this book is available
from the British Library.

ISBN-13: 978-0-7153-2377-9
ISBN-10: 0-7153-2377-6

Printed in China by RR Donnelly
for David & Charles
Brunel House   Newton Abbot   Devon

Commissioning Editor   Mic Cady
Editor Ame Verso
Project Editor   Marilynne Lanng
Researcher   Laura Gil Lasheras
Head of Design   Prudence Rogers
Designers   Charly Bailey and Lisa Wyman
Production Controller   Ros Napper

Visit our website at www.davidandcharles.co.uk

David & Charles books are available from all
good bookshops; alternatively you can contact
our Orderline on 0870 9908222 or write to us
at FREEPOSTEX2 110, D&C Direct, Newton
Abbot, TQ12 4ZZ (no stamp required UK only);
US customers call 800-289-0963 and Canadian
customers call 800-840-5220.

Contents

Using this Book

Defining castles

Best Castles includes descriptions of more than a hundred castles in England, Scotland, Wales and Ireland. The definition of the word 'castle' is generally taken to be a fortified military residence. In this respect they are considered to be different to their British precursors, hill forts, Roman forts and Saxon burhs, for example. All of these were military establishments but they were not usually also places to live in permanently. Some hill forts were undoubtedly lived in, but here the distinction is that they were communal in their purpose, whereas castles were built for, and owned by, one individual and his family and retainers, rather than the wider community. However, not all the castles described in this book fit into a neat category; they have been included to provide a fuller picture.

Providing more information

As well as describing the castles as architecture, in most cases background information is provided. Especially important or interesting castles are given more space and more background information. You might find that these castles are out of their true alphabetical order in the listings, but you can locate them by using the index. In order to help provide context, the book has a key dates and events list on pages 8–11, and a series of introductory features on pages 12–19. There are also ten special features on such subjects as Life in Early Castles, Food and Drink, Weapons, and so forth, throughout the book. Finally, a glossary of architectural terms can be found on page 186.

The castles included

A carefully chosen selection of the most historic, interesting and exciting castles is included in this book. For a more comprehensive gazetteer of castles see *Castles* (D&C, 2005) upon which this book is based. The publisher would be delighted to hear from readers who wish to provide more information or who think that other castles should be added.

Opening times/access information

Opening times and other useful information is included for the castles in this book, but please be aware that such information is subject to change, and therefore the publishers cannot accept responsibility if the information provided has changed. In as many cases as possible we have provided telephone numbers and website addresses, and visitors may wish to check details before planning a visit. In addition, full contact information for organizations such as the National Trust, English Heritage, Historic Scotland, Cadw and the Office of Public Works is included on page 192.

By their nature, castles often have areas where visitors – especially those with children – should exercise caution and the publishers cannot accept responsibility for any accident or other event as a result of using this book.

Locations and map references

If the castle is in the village or town that has its name the location information is limited to its county or statutory area (see map opposite). If it is in a very small settlement, or in the countryside, the nearest village or town is named.

Every entry is provided with a national grid map reference. All reputable large-scale maps – especially those from the Ordnance Survey organizations of Britain and Ireland – include the grid, and accurate locations can be plotted.

Counties Map

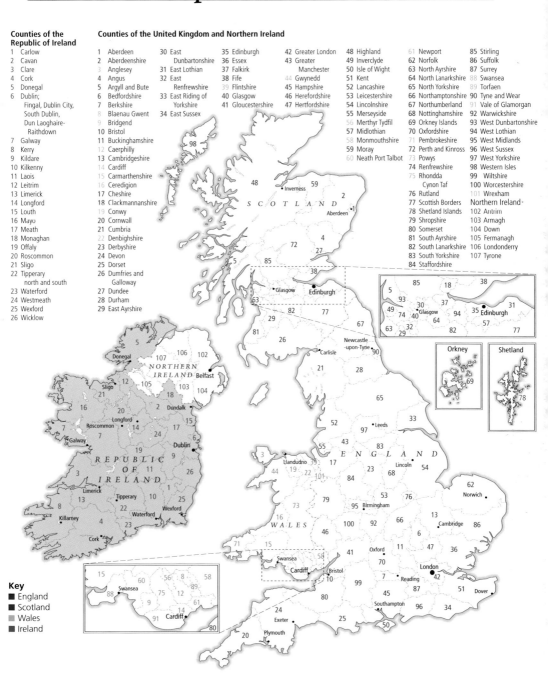

Counties of the Republic of Ireland

1 Carlow
2 Cavan
3 Clare
4 Cork
5 Donegal
6 Dublin;
   Fingal, Dublin City,
   South Dublin,
   Dun Laoghaire-
   Raithdown
7 Galway
8 Kerry
9 Kildare
10 Kilkenny
11 Laois
12 Leitrim
13 Limerick
14 Longford
15 Louth
16 Mayo
17 Meath
18 Monaghan
19 Offaly
20 Roscommon
21 Sligo
22 Tipperary
   north and south
23 Waterford
24 Westmeath
25 Wexford
26 Wicklow

Counties of the United Kingdom and Northern Ireland

1 Aberdeen
2 Aberdeenshire
3 Anglesey
4 Angus
5 Argyll and Bute
6 Bedfordshire
7 Berkshire
8 Blaenau Gwent
9 Bridgend
10 Bristol
11 Buckinghamshire
12 Caerphilly
13 Cambridgeshire
14 Cardiff
15 Carmarthenshire
16 Ceredigion
17 Cheshire
18 Clackmannanshire
19 Conwy
20 Cornwall
21 Cumbria
22 Denbighshire
23 Derbyshire
24 Devon
25 Dorset
26 Dumfries and
   Galloway
27 Dundee
28 Durham
29 East Ayrshire

30 East
   Dunbartonshire
31 East Lothian
32 East
   Renfrewshire
33 East Riding of
   Yorkshire
34 East Sussex
35 Edinburgh
36 Essex
37 Falkirk
38 Fife
39 Flintshire
40 Glasgow
41 Gloucestershire

42 Greater London
43 Greater
   Manchester
44 Gwynedd
45 Hampshire
46 Herefordshire
47 Hertfordshire
48 Highland
49 Inverclyde
50 Isle of Wight
51 Kent
52 Lancashire
53 Leicestershire
54 Lincolnshire
55 Merseyside
56 Merthyr Tydfil
57 Midlothian
58 Monmouthshire
59 Moray
60 Neath Port Talbot

61 Newport
62 Norfolk
63 North Ayrshire
64 North Lanarkshire
65 North Yorkshire
66 Northamptonshire
67 Northumberland
68 Nottinghamshire
69 Orkney Islands
70 Oxfordshire
71 Pembrokeshire
72 Perth and Kinross
73 Powys
74 Renfrewshire
75 Rhondda
   Cynon Taf
76 Rutland
77 Scottish Borders
78 Shetland Islands
79 Shropshire
80 Somerset
81 South Ayrshire
82 South Lanarkshire
83 South Yorkshire
84 Staffordshire

85 Stirling
86 Suffolk
87 Surrey
88 Swansea
89 Torfaen
90 Tyne and Wear
91 Vale of Glamorgan
92 Warwickshire
93 West Dunbartonshire
94 West Lothian
95 West Midlands
96 West Sussex
97 West Yorkshire
98 Western Isles
99 Wiltshire
100 Worcestershire
101 Wrexham

Northern Ireland
102 Antrim
103 Armagh
104 Down
105 Fermanagh
106 Londonderry
107 Tyrone

Key
■ England
■ Scotland
■ Wales
■ Ireland

Key Dates

Castles are a product of their times, and of the dominant personalities of those times. For much of British and Irish history, it is the monarch who is the most important single influence on events – for good or ill. By their nature, castles date from times of war, insecurity and danger. As peace and security become the norm, castles are either abandoned or adapted for more peaceful times.

The key events set out below are intended to help put castles into their historical context. Included are dates and events from English, Scottish, Welsh and Irish history, but this is not intended to be a full summary of the history of the four countries, and there are fewer events as castles decline in importance. The list includes English, Scottish and some Irish kings, and the early Welsh princes; their years as monarchs are in bold.

Key
- England
- Scotland
- Wales
- Ireland

- **43AD–411** Roman conquest of Britain
- **432** St Patrick arrives in Ireland
- **871–899 Alfred the Great**
- **1002–1014 Brian Bórú**
- **1039–1063 Gruffydd ap Llywelyn ap Seisyll**
- **1042–1066 Edward** (the Confessor)
- **1058–1093 Malcolm III**
- **1063–1075 Bleddyn ap Cynfyn**
- **1066 Harold II**
- **1066 September** Battle of Stamford Bridge
- **1066 September** William the Conqueror lands in Britain
- **1066 October** Battle of Hastings
- **1066–1087 William I**
- **1067** Chepstow Castle
- **1068** Warwick Castle
- **1069–1070** Harrying of the North
- **1075–1081 Trahaern ap Caradog**
- **1076** Colchester Castle begun

- **1078** White Tower, Tower of London completed
- **1080** Cardiff Castle
- **1080** Windsor Castle
- **1080** Domesday Survey ordered
- **1081–1137 Gruffydd ap Cynan ap Iago**
- **1087–1100 William II**
- **1093** Battle of Alnwick – Malcolm III of Scotland and his son Edward killed
- **1093–1097 Donald III**
- **1095** Council of Rockingham
- **1096** Alnwick Castle begun
- **1097–1107 Edgar**
- **1100–1135 Henry I**
- **1107–1124 Alexander I**
- **1124–1153 David I**
- **1127** Rochester Castle keep begun
- **1135–1154 Stephen**
- **1137–1170 Owain Gwynedd**
- **1138–1148** Civil war between Stephen and Matilda

- **1138** Scots invade Northumberland
- **1138 August** Battle of the Standard – Scots are defeated
- **1140** Hedingham Castle
- **1141** Stephen captured by Matilda's forces at Battle of Lincoln. Matilda elected Queen of England. Later in year Stephen released.
- **1146** Giraldis Cambrensis born at Pembroke
- **1148** Matilda leaves England
- **1153–1165 Malcolm IV**
- **1154–1189 Henry II**
- **1165–1214 William I**
- **1165** Orford Castle begun
- **1166–1175 Ruaidhrí Ó Conchubhair**
- **1170–1195 Dafydd ap Owain Gwynedd**
- **1170** Murder of Thomas Becket at Canterbury
- **1170** Normans arrive in Co. Wexford: Richard de Clare, Earl of Pembroke (Strongbow) comes to Ireland
- **1171** Strongbow becomes King of Leinster. Henry II visits Ireland
- **1173** Trim Castle
- **1173** Henry's son and the barons revolt against Henry II
- **1174** Battle of Alnwick. William I invades northern England in support of barons' rebellion against Henry II. William captured and forced to accept Henry II as superior.
- **1185** Prince John (later King John) created Lord of Ireland
- **1189–1199 Richard I** (the Lionheart)
- **1189–1200** Framlingham Castle rebuilt
- **1194–1240 Llywelyn Fawr** (Llywelyn the Great)
- **1199–1216 John**

- **1210** Submission of Irish kings to John
- **1214–1216** Barons' Revolt
- **1214–1249 Alexander II**
- **1215** Magna Carta
- **1216–1272 Henry III**
- **1216** Prince Louis of France invades England
- **1217** Battle of Lincoln between armies of Henry III and Louis. Louis defeated
- **1240–1246 Dafydd ap Llywelyn**
- **1246–1282 Llywelyn ap Gruffydd ap Llywelyn**
- **1249–1286 Alexander III**
- **1264–1267** Barons' War
- **1264** Battle of Lewes
- **1265** Battle of Evesham – Simon de Montfort killed
- **1266** Hebrides and Isle of Man given to Scots by King of Norway
- **1268** Caerphilly Castle begun
- **1272–1307 Edward I**
- **1277** Edward begins his war on Wales. In December Edward defeats Llywelyn ap Gruffudd ap Llywelyn
- **1277** Flint Castle, the first of Edward's iron ring
- **1283** Caernarvon, Conway and Harlech Castles begun
- **1284** Statute of Wales: Wales comes under Direct Rule
- **1286–1290 Margaret**
- **1290–1292** First Interregnum
- **1292–1296 John Balliol**
- **1295** The Auld Alliance
- **1295** Beaumaris Castle
- **1295–1363** Scottish Wars of Independence
- **1296** Battle of Dunbar (between Balliol and Edward I)
- **1297** Battle of Stirling Bridge

- **1298** Battle of Falkirk – Wallace defeated
- **1296–1306** Second Interregnum
- **1306–1329 Robert I (the Bruce)**
- **1307** Battle of Loudoun Hill
- **1307–1327 Edward II**
- **1312** Piers Gaveston executed
- **1314** Battle of Bannockburn
- **1315** Edward Bruce invades Ireland. Edward proclaimed King of Ireland.
- **1316–1318 Éadbhard I (Edward)**
- **1326** Execution of Hugh Despenser
- **1327–1377 Edward III**
- **1329–1371 David II**
- **1337–1453** Hundred Years' War
- **1346** Battle of Neville's Cross
- **1348** Black Death arrives in England
- **1348** Foundation of the Order of the Garter at Windsor
- **1358** Death of Queen Isabella.
- **1371–1390 Robert II**
- **1376** Edward the Black Prince dies
- **1366** Statutes of Kilkenny
- **1377–1399 Richard II**
- **1381** Peasants' Revolt
- **1385** Bodiam Castle
- **1390–1406 Robert III**
- **1399** Richard II goes to Ireland
- **1399** Richard II imprisoned at Pontefract Castle
- **1399–1413 Henry IV**
- **1400–1409** Owain Glyn Dwr's Revolt
- **1403–1409** Percys' Revolt
- **1403** Battle of Shrewsbury
- **1406–1437 James I**
- **1408** Battle of Bramham Moor

- **1413–1422 Henry V**
- **1422–1461 Henry VI**
- **1437–1460 James II**
- **1441** Herstmonceux – one of first castles built in brick, along with Caister
- **1453–1485** Wars of the Roses
- **1460–1488 James III**
- **1460** Battle of Wakefield
- **1461–1470 Edward IV**
- **1461** Battle of Mortimer's Cross
- **1470–1471 Henry VI**
- **1471 April** Battle of Barnet: death of Richard Neville, Earl of Warwick
- **1471 May** Battle of Tewkesbury: death of Edward, Prince of Wales
- **1471–1483 Edward IV**
- **1483 Edward V** – one of the princes allegedly murdered in the Tower of London
- **1483–1485 Richard III**
- **1485** Battle of Bosworth Field
- **1485–1509 Henry VII**
- **1488** Battle of Sauchieburn
- **1488–1513 James IV**
- **1499** Execution of Perkin Warbeck
- **1509–1547 Henry VIII**
- **1511** Thornbury Castle, England's last important fortified manor built
- **1513–1542 James V**
- **1513** Battle of Flodden Field
- **1534** Act of Supremacy
- **1536–1540** Dissolution of the Monasteries
- **1536** Pilgrimage of Grace
- **1536** Act of Union with Wales
- **1541–1547 Henry VIII King of Ireland**
- **1542–1567 Mary, Queen of Scots**

- **1542** Battle of Solway Moss
- **1543–1548** Rough Wooing
- **1547–1553 Edward VI**
- **1547** Battle of Pinkie
- **1553–1558 Mary I**
- **1554** Mary marries Philip of Spain
- **1558–1603 Elizabeth I**
- **1560** Treaty of Edinburgh
- **1567–1625 James VI**
- **1567–1573** Scottish Civil War
- **1569** Rising of the North
- **1573** Fall of Edinburgh Castle
- **1587** Execution of Mary, Queen of Scots at Fotheringhay Castle
- **1588** Spanish Armada
- **1594–1603** Nine Years' War
- **1603–1625 James I** (Union of the Crowns of Scotland and England; end of the war with Spain)
- **1605** Gunpowder Plot
- **1609–1613** Plantation of Ulster
- **1625–1649 Charles I**
- **1641–1648** Irish Rebellion of 1641 and Confederate Wars
- **1642–1646** English Civil War
- **1648–1651** English Civil War
- **1649–1660** The Commonwealth
- **1649** Start of Cromwell's campaign in Ireland
- **1649–1685 Charles II**
- **1653** Cromwell's Act of Settlement
- **1660** Restoration of the Monarchy
- **1660–1685 Charles II**
- **1666** Great Fire of London
- **1678** Lethendy Tower built, one of the last tower houses in Scotland

- **1685–1688 James II (VII of Scotland)**
- **1688** Glorious Revolution
- **1689–1745** Jacobite uprisings
- **1689–1702 William III & Mary**
- **1689–1694 Mary II**
- **1689 – 90** James II flees to Ireland
- **1690** Battle of the Boyne
- **1702–1714 Anne**
- **1707** Act of Union with Scotland
- **1714–1727 George I**
- **1727–1760 George II**
- **1746** Battle of Culloden Moor – last military battle on British soil
- **1746** Blair Castle besieged – last siege of a castle in Britain
- **1760–1820 George III**
- **1798** Wolfe Tone's Rebellion
- **1800** Ireland Act of Union
- **1803–1815** Napoleonic Wars
- **1820–1830 George IV**
- **1830–1837 William IV**
- **1837–1901 Victoria**
- **1901–1910 Edward VII**
- **1910–1936 George V**
- **1914–1918** World War I
- **1919–1921** Anglo–Irish War
- **1921** Anglo–Irish Treaty
- **1914–1918** World War I
- **1936** Abdication of **Edward VIII**
- **1936–1952 George VI**
- **1939–1945** World War II – last active use of castles on British soil
- **1952–present Elizabeth II**

Early Fortifications

Castles are defined as buildings with two primary purposes: places of defence and attack, and places in which to live. And they belonged to a particular individual, unlike prehistoric forts, for example, which were communal in their purpose and function.

The idea of castles grew out of the fortifications that men had used for centuries. In England, some of the most conspicuous of these are the great hill forts built in the Iron Age. Outstanding examples of these are Maiden Castle and Hod Hill in Dorset, and Danebury in Hampshire. These monuments consist of enormous earthen ramparts, originally topped by wooden walls and walkways, and surrounded by deep ditches. Some of these were only used at certain times of the year, or during periods of war, but at Danebury, for example, excavations have revealed the remains of hundreds of huts, as well as other features, including thousands of pits used for storing grain. Such forts were at the core of highly organized and sophisticated tribal societies.

It was the Roman invasion that sounded the death-knell for hill forts. The Romans overran them with comparative ease despite their defences, and the kind of society the Romans introduced revolved around towns. Almost all the ancient hill forts were abandoned. An exception is Old Sarum, the precursor of Salisbury in Wiltshire. Here the hill fort was re-used several times and abandoned only in the 13th century.

Roman military fortifications were built with typical efficiency. Even temporary marching camps were well built, with many still surviving. Such camps could be built at the end of each day's advance, as a base for future advances, or as a place to fall back to.

After the Romans left, some of the old hill forts were re-occupied, including Cadbury in Somerset, which some think may have been the headquarters of King Arthur. A systematic fortification-building programme was undertaken in the 9th century by King Alfred to counter attacks by Vikings. Called burhs, these forts were highly effective when manned by determined troops.

The Normans introduced the fortifications that we know as castles. They based these on structures in use on the European mainland since at least the 9th century. Within a short time of the invasion, Norman castles were built all over the British Isles; they were to become the symbol of Norman might and conquest, and were the focus of great historical events for the next 700 years.

Dun Aenghus, Ireland: promontory forts like this exist in large numbers along the coast of Ireland, and there are some on the British coast. Typically built of drystone walling, they could easily be defended, but there was no easy escape for the defenders if their attackers broke through.

Building Castles

The Normans built their wooden motte and bailey castles to help conquer in purely military terms, but the stone castles that followed were intended to dominate in psychological ways as well. London's White Tower is a perfect example. It was begun in 1070 specifically to intimidate the people of the city. Nothing like these immense stone structures had been seen in Britain before.

Castles were a central element of the feudal system: they belonged to the lords who built them. The king granted the lords land and other benefits; in return the lords paid fealty and service. Within their fiefdoms the lords could do pretty much as they pleased. For example, the Marcher Lords – William FitzOsbern at Hereford, Roger of Montgomery at Shrewsbury and 'Fat' Hugh 'The Wolf' of Avranches based at Chester – held complete sway along the whole Welsh border and made raids deep into Wales itself.

FitzOsbern's castle at Chepstow was the first purpose-built stone castle in Wales and said one thing: control. But Wales did not give up without a struggle. There had been resistance against the Normans ('the French' as Welsh chroniclers called them) since their arrival. In 1094 there was an uprising across the country that amounted to open war.

There were similar uprisings in the North; the reprisals were as fast and merciless. The Norman lords made excursions into Scotland, and Richard FitzGilbert de Clare – 'Strongbow' – mounted vicious campaigns in Ireland. Strongbow's actions reverberated down through the centuries of Ireland's history and his name is still reviled in parts of the country.

Wherever the lords came they had to build castles – for defence, to regroup in, to hold provisions in, and to rule from. And castles were also home to the lord's family and close retainers. As the first wooden castles were replaced by more permanent and secure structures of stone, so there were opportunities to introduce some degree of comfort and architectural improvements. Some of these ideas came from the religious wars we know as the Crusades. The Crusader castles – symbols of Christian religious imperialism in the Muslim world – were of stone and had to withstand attacks and the depredations of weather for a long time. They were far from easy support and supply chains, so had to be strong and self-contained. Castle builders applied what they learned during the Crusades and elsewhere to mighty fortresses all over the British Isles.

There are many natural defensive spurs and hills in Wales, good places to build castles. Welsh-built Castell-y-Bere is built on such a rocky outcrop. The native Welsh would not surrender to Norman rule, and so castles such as this were at the heart of a bloody struggle, and often changed hands.

Later Castles

Castles played a vital role in medieval history. They were the strong places from which attacks and rebellions were begun, and they were the refuges that offered protection when needed. Castles were built and destroyed often, and many of the castles in this book were already ruins in medieval times. Sometimes they remained in ruins because their strategic value had diminished; sometimes it was because their owners and their families could not afford to repair them, or were dead.

Castles in disputed regions were particularly vulnerable, obviously, and it was in these areas that there were most castles. It is no coincidence that some of the mightiest castles in Britain are in Wales, which fought against 'foreign' rule from the time of the Norman Conquest through to the 15th century. It was not until 1485, when Henry Tudor defeated Richard III at the Battle of Bosworth, that Wales looked for peace with its neighbour, for Henry had Welsh blood, and became the first 'Welsh' king of England.

Scotland and Ireland were also frequently at open war with the English. Like Wales, Scotland's rugged and wild landscapes aided

Bolton Castle, Yorkshire. Master-mason John Lewyn built it for Richard le Scrope, 1st Lord Bolton, in 1399. It was adapted and rebuilt many times in succeeding centuries, becoming a document in stone for the history it lived through. It was besieged during the Civil War, holding out for over a year. The Bolton family played a key role in British history, and the castle still belongs to them, an example of historical continuity that makes its story all the more remarkable.

The ruins of Coity Castle, in South Wales: during the course of 500 years it developed from a simple earthwork fortification to a complex set of buildings. It fell into ruins in the 17th century.

its native warriors. They could behave like guerrilla fighters, disappearing into the mountain fastnesses when they wanted to. But castles played a key role here, as well. They guarded the important towns, ports and passes, and some became the strongholds of the Scottish clans. Scottish leaders sought help from many quarters in their struggles with the English, often bringing soldiers in from elsewhere in Europe, and these fighters brought with them new ideas on castle design from the Continent.

The wars in Ireland were among the most bloody and prolonged in the British Isles, and left a legacy of bitterness that could still be detected in the Irish 'troubles' of the 20th century. The visible legacy is hundreds of castles littered across the landscape. Until very recently most of these were half-forgotten ivy-covered ruins, but Ireland's new wealth is helping to restore many of them, often as private homes.

Eilean Donan is the traditional Scottish castle home of the MacRae clan. Originally built in the 13th century, it was left in ruins after bombardment by warships in 1719. It was restored in the first half of the 20th century, and is now well known for its many appearances in films.

Perhaps the most impressive single group of castles in the British Isles is that in North Wales. The most well known are Caernarfon, Conwy, Beaumaris and Harlech, but a dozen others were also either newly built or rebuilds of existing castles. All were the architectural brainchild of Master James of St Georges, whom Edward I had met in Savoy. The two men worked together to plan a 'ring' of castles that would put an end to resistance in Wales. It was an extraordinary undertaking, involving thousands of workers over a 25-year period and with a total cost of something like £40 million ($70 million) in contemporary terms.

A Variety of Roles

As English society became more settled, so the role of castles as places of defence and offence became less important. In unruly Scotland and Ireland they were still needed, as much as a protection from internecine strife as for anything else. More and more castles became royal property and royal residences. This underlined the fact that the central authority was the monarchy. And they were essential to house the monarch and his huge retinue as he travelled around.

Comfort became much more important, and castles became less forbidding. At the same time, new forms of weaponry meant that castle architecture had to change again and again if it was to keep up with innovative attack methods. Cannons and similar ordnance were a particular challenge in that these increasingly powerful weapons could inflict devastating damage on even the strongest castle if the gunners were skilled and determined enough. To counter such threats, castles were adapted to be equipped with platforms for cannons that could fire back at the assaulting ordnance.

Water was one of the best ways of deterring 'sappers', whose job it was to undermine castle walls by tunnelling under them. A breadth of water, a moat, made any such tunnel longer, and if the water broke through, the sappers would probably be drowned.

Towers have always been at the heart of castle design, and tower castles and houses were built in very large numbers in Ireland and Scotland. Scotland's Castle Stalker has the added protection of being built on an island, and has mainly been reached by boat. It originally belonged to the Stewart clan, but passed to the Campbells in the 17th century. Descendants of the original Stewart owners regained it at the beginning of the 20th century.

Edward I's 'ring' of castles in North Wales inspired much innovation: the emphasis was on the outer walls and gatehouses and on enormous defensive structures such as waterworks that went well beyond the idea of a mere moat.

Castles built in the 14th and 15th centuries often looked formidable on the outside, but were essentially domestic in their function inside. Good examples of this are at Bodiam and Herstmonceux. In such castles, the all-important great hall (the setting for virtually all gatherings and meals) could now have large windows, built as it was against the outer walls, with its windows facing into the central courtyard. All the other necessary domestic buildings were protected within the outer walls, including kitchens, ovens, store rooms, cellars and so on. One of the best places to see some of these arrangements is within the shattered ruins of Basing House in Hampshire, where the interior domestic arrangements take on a special poignancy because large numbers of its defenders were trapped and burned to death here in the Civil War siege that

The design of Caernarfon strongly resembles Constantinople, which Edward saw when he was on the Crusades. He used the town as part of his defensive system and it, too, was enclosed within fortified walls with towers all round.

resulted in its eventual total destruction.

Whole towns were often included within defensive structures centred round the castle. Excellent survivals include Edward's Caernarfon and Conwy. In Southampton, the castle has all but disappeared under modern housing, but the formidable town walls, built to protect the city from attack by sea, still stand to their full height in places. They incorporate much of interest, including exciting survivors of Norman domestic architecture. At York, the circuit along the top of the town walls is one of the best ways of exploring the city.

Long after they ceased to have a practical function, castles were often kept by their owners for sentimental or historical reasons. Indeed, there are castles in Britain and Ireland still owned by the families that built them 600 or 700 years ago.

The End of the Castle

Castles gradually ceased to have a defensive role throughout much of the British Isles as society became more settled and secure. But castles came into their own again during the Civil War of the 17th century. As a result, many were destroyed in sieges, and many more were destroyed by both sides so they could not be used again. A prime example is Corfe Castle in Dorset (see page 46), 'slighted' by the Parliamentarians after a long siege.

The Civil War also brought changes in the nature of what a defensive position was – thick, earth banks with a low profile were actually more effective protection against cannon fire than tall castle walls. Plans and

drawings of the time show how sophisticated such fortifications could be.

Such ideas were not new, however. Henry VIII had been forced to build new kinds of fortresses along the coast of England as a result of threats of invasion from France and Spain. These were built from scratch with artillery in mind – both from attackers and for defence. Deal, Walmer and Sandown were built on a 2km (3-mile) stretch in Kent to protect a vital safe anchorage between the Goodwin Sands and the coast. Of these Deal is the best preserved, and shows to perfection the ideas of artillery-based fortifications: low, thick, rounded towers serve as platforms for heavy guns, while lighter guns can be fired from the ports which pierce the towers. Similar 'castles' (they are forts, really) were built to protect many other vulnerable anchorages and ports. These include Pendennis in Cornwall (see page 68), which was later refortified with the type of angled bastions along its outer walls that were to become the norm for the next 300 years.

A martello tower off the coast of Ireland on the island called Ireland's Eye. Martello towers were all built to a similar pattern. A single cannon was originally placed on a rotating platform on the roof, and the roof was very thick to protect from mortar fire. The body of the tower housed a garrison of men, along with their provisions and ammunition.

Another key example of new thinking in defence is the town walls of Berwick-upon-Tweed. Here, triangular bastions deflect enemy fire and enable crossfire from all angles. At Fort George in Inverness, there are very similar bastions, although these were built nearly 200 years after the walls at Berwick.

Towers have always been an important part of defensive design. There are hundreds of examples to be seen in Scotland and Ireland, with many still in use today as homes. They were practical structures used for defence until the 16th century and beyond. Later ones were built with guns very much in mind, as the array of gun ports at Dunnottar Castle in Scotland shows.

In the 19th century towers came back into fashion as defensive structures as a response to the threat of invasion from France in the Napoleonic Wars. More than a hundred were eventually built, but their guns never fired a shot in anger or defence. New developments in artillery technology – rifled barrels firing metal shells – rendered all such defences virtually useless, but in the 1860s new forts were once again built all round the coast of England. These included the last great fortifications ever built in the British Isles. Some were armour plated to withstand artillery attack.

The last threatened invasion of Britain by sea came in World War II. The answer was to refortify many of the coastal fortifications sometimes built hundreds of years before, and included the construction of thousands of pillboxes.

These tiny concrete boxes housed machine-gun emplacements, and were often cleverly and effectively disguised as such things as ice-cream kiosks, haystacks and even piles of logs. A far cry from the great castles of the likes of Edward I, they were the correct response to the ever-changing nature of war.

At Dunnottar Castle the wall nearest the mainland was equipped with gun ports, despite its conversion to a palatial residence in the late 16th century.

The battered walls of Swansea Castle framed against the shining glass of a modern office block. Whether pristine or ruined, in town or overgrown in the countryside, castles have a powerful attraction and the ability to conjure the past.

England

Many castles in England now stand in neat lawns and among colourful flowerbeds. On sunny days they are the epitome of romance. But this disguises their often bloody and violent past.

Some of the most important castles in England are still in use – Windsor and the Tower of London are the most famous examples. A number are still lived in by the descendants of those who built them, sometimes 500 or more years ago. Some ruined ones drowse in remote rural settings, perhaps unrecognized even by locals. They are a central part of the story of England, and often of significant architectural importance.

Alnwick

One of the best-known castles in Britain, its current popularity partly attributable to its starring role in the Harry Potter films, Alnwick's history is as interesting as any work of fiction. The castle is still the seat of the Dukes of Northumberland and is the second-largest inhabited castle in the country.

History

Yves de Vescy built the earliest parts of the fortress in 1096 and by the middle of the 12th century the castle had taken on the basic plan that remains today. It was one of the earliest Norman fortresses to have been built without a square keep, and fragments of the Norman masonry still exist in the curtain walls.

The de Vescys held Alnwick through several sieges and periods of turbulence (Eustace de Vescy was a ringleader of the Barons' Revolt in 1212; the castle was ordered to be destroyed, but this wasn't carried out) until early in the 14th century when the fortress and manors of Alnwick were handed to Anthony Bek,

Bishop of Durham. The direct male line of the de Vescys died out in 1314 at the Battle of Bannockburn and the de Percy family, who became one of England's most powerful dynasties, came to Alnwick in 1309.

The de Percys

The de Percys were already important English landowners when Henry de Percy bought the castle. Henry, the 1st Lord Percy of Alnwick, started to transform the castle into a formidable stronghold and palatial residence: he reconstructed the keep and rebuilt most of the towers on the curtain wall. His son continued the reconstruction – the octagonal towers on either side of the keep's entrance are his and date from *c*.1350. Generations of de Percys made their mark on Alnwick but during the second half of the 18th century Robert Adam altered the castle in the Gothic Revival style (much of this work was later removed). Around the same time Alnwick first became home to the Dukes of Northumberland.

The de Percy family and Alnwick were often intertwined with many of the pivotal events of British history. Contemporary invaders of Alnwick are the visitors who come to view this important part of the nation's heritage and to be reminded of the ancestry of the present 12th Duke of Northumberland, Ralph Percy.

Today

Today the castle receives around 300,000 visitors and is becoming recognized as a must-see destination nationally and internationally. There certainly is plenty here to occupy visitors of all ages. The Harry Potter link will engage many children and, one day a week in the summer, Hagrid and Professor Dumbledore are on hand to perform magic. The Knight's School allows youngsters to experience what it was like to train as a knight. Also in summer a magician performs tricks and birds of prey are demonstrated. Alnwick's website offers lots of games and fun for kids. If you feel like a break for refreshments, there is a tea room.

The castle is filled with treasures, including paintings by artists such as Bellini, Gainsborough and Claude Lorraine, furniture and statues accumulated by the family and it has its own museum. Events are staged regularly and there are permanent displays to further your knowledge about the castle and the part it played in history.

The Alnwick Garden

Outside, the duchess has supervised the transformation of an area of disused land into the Alnwick Garden, a reason in its own right for a visit. The garden, a charity, operates separately from the castle; for information, visit its website, www.alnwickgarden.com.

Location	Northumberland
Map ref	NU 187137
Tel	01665 510777 or 01665 511100 (24hrs)
Web	www.alnwickcastle.com
Open	Apr–late Oct daily 11–5

Arundel

At first sight, Arundel is a neo-Gothic Victorian castle, an impression created by the monumental restoration and rebuilding project started at the end of the 19th century. But much of Arundel's Norman and medieval inheritance still exists in its palatial structure.

History

Arundel's origins go back to the earliest years of the Conquest when Roger de Montgomery was created Earl of Arundel. De Montgomery's only legacy at Arundel is the motte, which, at over 30m (100ft), dominates the centre of the site and would have been topped with timber fortifications, which were replaced less than a century later with stone. The lowest part of the inner gatehouse and an adjacent stretch of curtain wall (c.1070) are remnants of these early stone defences. The rest of the curtain, built of local flint and enclosing the whole site, was erected in stages between the 12th and 13th centuries. Henry I's widow, Adeliza of Louvain and her new husband, William d'Albini, were responsible for the windowless stone keep built on the motte in 1138. It was under Henry II's aegis that the medieval fortress was further enhanced.

The Fitzalan Howards

From that time the castle and lands at Arundel descended directly and, more or less, without interruption from the 12th century through a line of d'Albinis, Fitzalans and Howards. Sometimes perilously, the Howard name has been up among the 'movers and shakers' of the day since Tudor times and, as staunch Roman Catholics, the family can claim a saint and two cardinals among their ancestors. The Catholic Fitzalan Chapel, founded in the 14th century, is, unusually, part of a structure that also serves as the Protestant parish church, the two parts divided by a glass wall. Famous for the artistry of the ancient noble tombs, this chapel is still the burial place of the Dukes of Norfolk.

The castle

Besieged twice, Arundel was badly damaged during the Civil War and slighted a decade later. Repairs weren't initiated until the 18th century when the 11th Duke, a friend of the Prince Regent and keen amateur architect, began the reconstruction. He created the park and built Hiorne's Tower, though the main survivor and highlight of his works is the mahogany-lined library, considered one of England's most important interiors from that period. However, it wasn't until the last years of the 19th century that the castle was brought to its current magnificence. The 15th Duke of Norfolk employed the architect and antiquarian, Charles Alban Buckler, to carry out extensive rebuilding and refurbishment. The castle they created is an affirmation of the finest Victorian craftsmanship incorporated with nearly a thousand years of the history of one of the greatest peerages in the land.

Furniture, tapestries and paintings from the magnificent collection amassed by 'the Collector Earl' in the 17th century are displayed inside the castle. Thomas, the 14th Earl of Arundel, was a patron of artists such as Inigo Jones, Rubens and van Dyck, whose portrait of the earl is displayed in the castle. Tours of the gardens, which include its history are led by the Head Gardener – details of dates are on the castle's website. The restaurant opens at 11am.

There is a lively calendar of events throughout the season and Saturday opening for special events (see the website).

Location	West Sussex
Map ref	TQ 019074
Tel	01903 882173
Web	www.arundelcastle.org
Open	Sun–Fri Apr–last Fri in Oct. Grounds 11–5, Castle 12–5 late Mar–Oct. Last admission 1 hour before closing

Ashby-de-la-Zouch

Ashby was a Norman hall begun in the 12th century but extended over the next three centuries to become a fair-sized manor house. In 1464 Edward IV passed it to his Lord Chamberlain, William, Lord Hastings. Hastings set about converting the manor into a castle after a licence was granted a decade later.

Hastings' Tower

The principal buildings of Hastings' time were the chapel and the great tower, known as Hastings' Tower. This formidable rectangular structure was a fortress-cum-residence and is unusual in two respects: most towers at the time were built to a cylindrical design, and it was set on the edge of the castle site rather than in the centre. The four-storey tower originally reached about 27.5m (90ft) to its semi-octagonal angle turrets with a seven-floor extension. Hastings Tower was blown in two during the Civil War but visitors can still enjoy fine views from the top of this majestic ruin.

History

Mary, Queen of Scots was kept at Ashby (pictured below) on two occasions and the castle features in the classic 19th-century novel, Sir Walter Scott's *Ivanhoe*.

Visiting the castle

As well as the fine views from the tower, visitors (with the aid of a torch) can explore an underground passage that was constructed during the war. Occasional events are held by English Heritage – check their website.

Location	Leicestershire
Map ref	SK 361166
Tel	01530 413343
Web	www.english-heritage.org.uk
Open	Daily 10–6 Jul–Aug; Thu–Mon 10–5 Sep–Oct, late Mar–Jun; Thu–Mon 10–4 Nov–Mar

Aydon

A wealthy Suffolk merchant built this fine example of a 13th-century manor house. Aydon was originally intended to be an undefended dwelling but was fortified early in the 14th century when troubles over border territories worsened. The castle was attacked by the Scots twice, in 1315 and again in 1346.

From the 17th century until the 1960s the castle was used as a farm but it has now been restored to its original medieval appearance.

What to do

Substantial parts of the original work survive and visitors can walk through the great hall, chambers, service rooms, and kitchen and servants' accommodation, seeing them just as they would have been in medieval times. Refreshments are available.

Location	Nr Corbridge, Northumberland
Map ref	NZ 001663
Tel	01434 632450
Web	www.english-heritage.org.uk
Open	Daily 10–6 late Mar–Sep

Barnard

Overlooking the Tees, Barnard Castle began as little more than a fortified enclosure of the late 11th century belonging to the Baliol family. It developed into a considerable oblong enclosure site divided into four stone-walled wards and, despite being little more than an imposing ruin today, was once one of the largest castles in the North. The most interesting feature of Barnard is its 13th-century cylindrical great tower built of sandstone blocks, which contrast with the rougher masonry of the curtain. Nearby lie the remains of a 13th- to 14th-century great hall.

History

When the castle was besieged by Alexander I of Scotland in 1216, Barnard was held by Hugh de Balliol. Much later in the century his grandson John became king of Scotland, but only for four years as John was deposed in 1296 and retired to his estates in Picardy. Barnard passed to the Bishop of Durham, but was claimed back by the Crown c.1300.

Later still the castle was owned by the Earls of Warwick and was kept on a strong defensive footing against attack from the Scots. During the Rising of the North in the 16th century, Barnard was besieged by 5,000 rebels and from then fell into a state of decay. Sir Henry Vane bought the castle in 1630; he dismantled the buildings and used the materials to build his grand residence at Raby.

Visiting the castle

The grounds of the castle include a sensory garden for visually impaired visitors. There are refreshments on site.

Location	Co. Durham
Map ref	NZ 049165
Tel	01833 638212
Web	www.english-heritage.org.uk
Open	Daily 10–6 late Mar–end Sep; daily 10–4 Oct; Mon, Thu–Sun 10–4 Nov–Mar

Bamburgh

Bamburgh, built by the Norman invaders in the 11th century, was an impregnable fortress and royal stronghold for around 400 years. In 1464, during the Wars of the Roses, this Lancastrian stronghold was the first English castle to fall to artillery ranged against it by the army of Edward IV. The earliest of the many sieges and skirmishes at the fortress came in 1095 when William II attacked Bamburgh using a siege-castle nicknamed Malvoisin (Evil Neighbour): the holder, Robert de Mowbray, was imprisoned for conspiring against the king, and from then until the early 17th century,

Bamburgh remained for the most part in royal hands, maintained as a fortress crucially sited for defence against Scottish invaders. Its great keep is attributed to Henry II and the fortress hosted many visits of the English monarchs.

The castle's structure

The castle's formidable outline is still silhouetted against the skyline, much as it would have been when it was one of the most important northern strongholds. Its current grandeur owes more to the 18th and 19th centuries. Bamburgh was ruinous

by the end of the 1600s with only the keep remaining intact. The 1st Lord Armstrong, a noteworthy industrialist, shipbuilder and engineer, purchased the property towards the end of the Victorian era, and he began massive reconstruction and restoration at the fortress.

Early history

Bamburgh's origins go far beyond the Norman castle. A British tribe owned the site in the 1st century BC. Then the Romans established a citadel here, and when they left Britain there is evidence that Bamburgh became the stronghold of a local chieftain. In AD547 Bamburgh was the seat of the Anglo-Saxon king, Ida. During the 7th century it came into the hands of Edwin of Northumbria, who brought the Roman missionary Paulinus to preach around Bamburgh. After Edwin's death, Oswald, the son of Edwin's adversary Ethelfrith, took Bamburgh and established a monastery on Lindisfarne (Holy Island) in 625; this became one of the world's great centres of learning, art and Christianity.

Museums

The castle houses two museums in the former laundry. The Armstrong Museum is dedicated to the life and work of the 1st Lord Armstrong while the Bamburgh Castle Aviation Artefacts Museum has aircraft from the 20th century, most notably from both world wars.

Location	Northumberland
Map ref	NU 184351
Tel	01668 214515
Web	www.bamburghcastle.com
Open	Daily 11–5 mid-Mar to Oct Last entry 30 mins before closing

Basing House

Basing House is famous for its role in the Civil War. It was built in 1535 on the site of a much earlier castle for the 1st Marquis of Winchester, Treasurer to Edward VI, Mary I and Elizabeth I. At the time it was the largest private house in the country.

The Civil War

When the Civil War broke out the 5th Marquis of Winchester defended Basing for the king, living up to his family motto *Aymez Loyaulte* (Love Loyalty); it is said that this was scratched on every windowpane of the house.

By 1645, despite attacks by the Parliamentarians on several occasions during a two-year-long siege, Basing was the last major Royalist garrison blocking the route to the west. In August that year around 800 Parliamentary troops launched an assault on the stronghold but the garrison held out. Reinforcements were sent and Cromwell himself joined the attacking force. It wasn't until October that a particularly heavy bombardment finally breached the walls and the ensuing ferocious battle overcame the defenders. Basing was razed to the ground although the earthworks and ruins make fascinating viewing.

The castle today

Archaeologists have uncovered the remains of a wing of the New House, previously thought to have been entirely lost. An exhibition helps to explain the events that led to the destruction of this interesting and substantial property. Civil War re-enactments usually take place each year.

Location	Nr Basingstoke, Hampshire
Map ref	SU 663526
Tel	01256 467295
Web	www.hants.gov.uk
Open	Wed–Sun 2–6, Apr–Sep

Beeston

In the early 12th century the site at Beeston belonged to the powerful Ranulf, Earl of Chester, who, *c*.1220, began to build the castle here. He designed the fortress in two parts, with a small inner bailey and an outer bailey surrounded by towers and walls and guarded by a massive gatehouse, but there was no keep.

History

In 1237 Beeston passed to Henry III, who enlarged it; and in the first years of the 14th century Edward I undertook major new works. However, during the following centuries, the castle became neglected and was in ruins by the 1500s.

Nevertheless, Beeston was garrisoned during the Civil War, first by Parliamentarians and then by Royalists, until it was finally slighted (intentionally destroyed).

Stone from the castle was used for buildings elsewhere but even in its present ruinous state, the castle's former strength is still detectable.

What to see

The climb up to the castle is very steep, but you will be rewarded with fine views. An exhibition, Castle of the Rock, explores the history of the site.

Location	Tarporley, Cheshire
Map ref	SJ 537593
Tel	01829 260464
Web	www.english-heritage.org.uk
Open	Daily 10–6 late Mar–Sep; daily 10–4 Oct–late Mar

Belvoir

Belvoir was first a motte castle built on a natural mound by Robert de Todeni in the late 11th century. The name, Belvoir, dates from this time and means 'beautiful view' but there is nothing now left of the original Norman castle.

A stately home

These days Belvoir is the grand stately home of the Duke of Rutland and it is the fourth building to stand on the original site.

The castle houses the Queen's Royal Lancers Museum and the stunning interiors include

Location	Leicestershire
Map ref	TL 296236
Tel	01476 871002
Web	www.belvoircastle.com
Open	Tue–Thu, Sat–Sun 11–5 Easter Sunday–Sep; Castle Sun, Grounds Sat–Sun 11–5 Mar & Oct. Telephone for details of closing on some Saturdays

magnificent collections of furniture, paintings, porcelains, silks and tapestries.

Berkeley

A motte castle was first built on this rising ground, which overlooks the plains between the Severn and the Cotswolds, by William FitzOsbern, one of William the Conqueror's commanders at Hastings.

Significant events

In the 1100s the site became the property of Robert FitzHarding, a supporter of Henry II and Provost of Bristol. He was granted permission to build a stone castle here. His huge shell keep, unusual in that it surrounds the motte, rather than perching on top, is one of the oldest surviving parts of the castle. Berkeley is famous as the site of the incarceration and murder of Edward II in 1327 as the result of a plot by his wife, Isabella of France, and Roger Mortimer. The castle was remodelled in the 14th century and is still in the possession of direct descendants of the FitzHardings.

A family home

Only superficially damaged in the Civil War, Berkeley Castle remains intact as a stately family home and retains many of its early features. Inside the castle, you can see the kitchens, which date from the 14th century, with items that span the centuries. Paintings, furniture, tapestries and silverware are on display in a number of rooms and halls. There is a tea room for refreshments.

Medieval fair

Some weekends each year are devoted to a medieval fair where the theme is jousting but there are other attractions, too, including music, cannon displays, a medieval market, a medieval hunt and the opportunity to try your hand at archery and other battle skills.

The gardens at Berkeley Castle are worth a visit in their own right. There are scented flowers to enjoy in June and rare shrubs and other plants throughout the grounds. Explore the grounds to discover more history and wonderful sights.

Location	Gloucestershire
Map ref	ST 685989
Tel	01453 810332
Web	www.berkeley-castle.com
Open	Fri–Sat, Mon 11–4, Sun 2–5 Easter; Tue–Sat 11–4, Sun 2–5 Apr–Sep; Sun 2–5 Oct (Butterfly House closed in Oct). Contact the castle or visit the website for additional information.

Berry Pomeroy

On a wooded hill close to the River Dart, this evocative ruin of a 16th-century fortified manor house enclosed by medieval defences has an unusual gatehouse with polygonal towers. Edward Seymour, Duke of Somerset and Protector of Edward VI, acquired the castle in 1547. Despite ambitious building projects Berry Pomeroy was abandoned by the Seymours at the beginning of the 18th century in favour of their country house in Somerset. Stripped of any valuable materials, the place was in ruins not long after. However, a wall of the gatehouse still carries a 15th-century painting of the Three Kings.

Things to do

Events are staged occasionally and the audio tour is very informative. There are a number of ghosts associated with Berry Pomeroy including the White Lady and the Blue Lady.

Location	Nr Totnes, Devon
Map ref	SX 839623
Tel	01803 866618
Web	www.english-heritage.org.uk
Open	Daily 10–5 late Mar–Jun, Sep; daily 10–6 Jul–Aug; daily 10–4 Oct

Bodiam

Conjure up an image of a storybook castle and it may well resemble Bodiam. This square fortress totally surrounded by a broad moat, seems to possess qualities that are both ethereal and monumentally solid. It was built towards the end of the 14th century, when castle design was shifting from serious and spartan towards greater comfort and aesthetics. Bodiam's perfect symmetry, created by stout drum towers at each corner and a postern, gatehouse and square interval towers inserted around the sides, is a curious mix of impenetrable fortress and manorial splendour.

Creator of Bodiam

Sir Edward Dalyngrigge, the castle's builder, was a wealthy man. His riches were accrued during the Hundred Years War when he

crossed the Channel in 1367 to fight alongside key figures in the long-running conflict with France. At one time he fought under Sir Robert Knollys, whose shield of arms is carved on the postern gate at Bodiam. Later, in the 1380s, as Knight of the Shire of Sussex, Dalyngrigge was a major player among the county's gentry. Internal unrest coupled with the belief that the south coast was under imminent threat of attack by the French, led Sir Edward to build a well-defended fortress. He obtained the licence to crenellate his existing mansion in October 1385 but instead chose a different, more strategic site to rebuild near a crossing on the River Rother. Bodiam's defences were effective but relatively simple: the ultra-wide moat was built to counteract mining under defensive walls, and further obstructions to attack included a series of three drawbridges, a powerful barbican and a gatehouse fully equipped with all manner of defensive tricks.

A famous ruin

Evidence shows that Bodiam was inhabited in some form up until the 17th century but by late in the 1700s the castle had become a celebrated ivy-clad ruin, inspiration for artists and architects.

Still enchanting, Bodiam's complete exterior is largely thanks to the restoration work carried out by Lord Curzon early in the last century and as a result you can explore the battlements and climb the spiral staircases in the towers to enjoy the view.

Location	East Sussex
Map ref	TQ 785256
Tel	01580 830436
Web	www.nationaltrust.org.uk
Open	Daily 10–6/dusk mid-Feb to Oct; Sat–Sun 10–4/ dusk Nov to mid-Feb

Bolsover

Bolsover was built in the 12th century and it received a great tower of stone *c*.1173–4. More domestic buildings were added in the 13th century but the castle was allowed to deteriorate during the reign of Edward I, when the buildings were leased. The castle you see today is the result of a building project Sir Charles Cavendish started in the 17th century. The 'Little Castle' he and his son built was designed purely for elegant living. The castle battlements have been renovated, and the wall paintings in the little castle have been restored. The Venus Garden with its fountain and statues is also now in full working order.

Location	Nr Chesterfield, Derbyshire
Map ref	SK 470707
Tel	01246 822844
Web	www.english-heritage.org.uk
Open	Thu–Mon 10–5 late Mar–Apr, Sep–Oct; daily 10–6 May–Aug; Thu–Mon 10–4 Nov–Mar. Closed Christmas and New Year. Closed on Sat at 4pm. Check website or telephone for times

Things to do

Sir Charles' son, William, built large stables to train horses and these have been converted into a discovery centre. Historical events, plays and concerts are staged at the castle, which also offers an audio tour and audio-visual displays. There is also a coffee shop.

Bolton

The considerable fortified manor house of Bolton Castle stands high on the north slope of Wensleydale. Granted a licence in 1379, Lord Scrope, Richard II's Chancellor had already begun to build a formidable quadrangle with substantial rectangular corner towers. The building work was undertaken by John Lewyn, a respected master mason, and the building contract for his work has survived. The castle was constructed from local stone, with quoins and arches in freestone, from a local quarry. Lord Scrope's quarters were separated from those accommodating his retainers. All doorways into the inner buildings from the courtyard were filled with portcullises. In Scrope's day the only entrance to the castle was a gatehouse in the eastern wing, protected by the southwest tower, which had a guardhouse at ground level. Mary, Queen of Scots was imprisoned here for six months in 1568.

Bolton was held for the king in the Civil War but was besieged for several months and surrendered to Parliament. It was slighted, leaving only parts of the castle suitable for accommodation. Periods of building work continued into the 20th century.

Visiting Bolton

Tableaux bring the past to life for visitors who can explore the castle's five floors. Re-enactments and living history events take place in summer and there are occasional children's days when youngsters can dress up and pretend they live in medieval times.

Bolton's medieval garden has been restored and the walled herb garden is planted with indigenous herbs. A tea room is open for refreshments.

Location	Castle Bolton, North Yorkshire
Map ref	SE 034918
Tel	01969 623981
Web	www.boltoncastle.com
Open	Daily 10–5 Apr–Oct; daily 10–4/dusk Nov–Mar

Brough

Brough Castle stands in one corner of the remains of the Roman fort of Verteris, guarding the routes south and across the Pennines against the Scots. The first work was a roughly triangular enclosure of stone begun late in the 11th century, making Brough one of the earliest castles in Britain to have stonework.

The Cliffords

During the mid-13th century the fortress was owned by the Clifford family who built a hall, tower and range of domestic buildings. Brough remained their family home until 1521 when it was ravaged by an accidental fire. Lady Anne Clifford restored the castle in the 17th century, but after she died Brough decayed and all that is left is an interesting ruin, though you can see the outline of Lady Anne's kitchen garden.

Location	Cumbria
Map ref	NY 791141
Tel	0870 333 1181
Web	www.english-heritage.org.uk
Open	Access at any reasonable time

Caister

Caister Castle, built between 1432 and 1446 by a self-made adventurer, Sir John Fastolf, was one of the first major brick buildings in England. Many details of the construction, materials, labour and costs have survived: one of these was a note of an attempt by one mason to overcharge for his work.

The great tower

The castle has a double enclosure in the form of two quadrangles surrounded entirely by water, but its principal feature was, and still is, the tall, slim, cylindrical great tower: it has five floors accessed via a spiral stairway and is equipped with machicolated parapet, gun ports and walls more than 1m (4ft) thick.

Points of interest

Caister was occupied for a time by the Paston family, whose letters (now in the British Museum) give a remarkable view of country life in the 15th century. An unlikely attraction at the castle is the country's largest private automobile collection, including the 1893 Panhard et Levassor.

Location	Nr Great Yarmouth, Norfolk
Map ref	TG 504123
Tel	01572 787251
Web	www.greateryarmouth.co.uk
Open	Sun–Fri 10–4.30 May–Sep

Carisbrooke

Carisbrooke was a fairly elaborate castle in its time. It started as a very early Norman motte castle built around 1070 by William FitzOsbern. Stonework was probably first added in the 12th century; the castle has a polygonal keep. One of its most notable features today is the gatehouse, dating from the 14th century.

Besieged in 1377 by a French commando force, Carisbrooke was also an important artillery fort in the 16th century, built in the face of possible Spanish attacks.

The castle today

Today the castle is most famous as the place where Charles I was held after he escaped from Hampton Court. Charles' rooms were in the great hall, which now houses a local history museum with displays relating to Charles' imprisonment and items found during excavations on the castle site. You can also explore the keep and battlements and see the working 16th-century well house, powered by donkeys. A tea room provides refreshments.

Location	Nr Newport, Isle of Wight
Map ref	SZ 486878
Tel	01983 522107
Web	www.english-heritage.org.uk
Open	Daily 10–5 late Mar–Sep; daily 10–4 Oct–Mar

Carlisle

The earliest castle structure at Carlisle was a wooden, palisaded enclosure, raised by William Rufus *c.*1092 on the high bluff overlooking the River Eden. Henry I is then recorded as having ordered a 'castle and towers' to be raised to fortify the city in 1122 and the first stone buildings were begun. The massive great tower was built later in the same century and is the oldest surviving part of the fortress.

Conflict and war

King David I of Scotland seized Carlisle Castle but Henry II reclaimed the castle in 1157. Its position, at the western end of the border with Scotland, ensured that this fortress was a frequent scene of conflict and change of ownership. Edward I renovated Carlisle and used it as his seat of government and headquarters when he invaded Scotland. Mary, Queen of Scots was held prisoner here following her abdication from the Scottish throne and the castle was also subjected to an eight-month siege when it was held by the Royalists during the Civil War. In 1746,

the final time Carlisle was involved in clashes, supporters of 'Bonnie' Prince Charlie had to defend the castle against the Hanoverian army.

History

In the keep, a room which was used as a prison during the Jacobite Rebellion, has the 'licking stones', so called because prisoners were driven by thirst to lick the stones to try to get some moisture from them. Carlisle continued to be used as barracks late into the 20th century and houses the museum of the King's Own Royal Border Regiment and much else of interest. The Carlisle Roman Dig, on the site, is an exhibition with objects from recent excavations. Events are held in the grounds.

Location	Cumbria
Map ref	NY 396562
Tel	01228 591992
Web	www.english-heritage.org.uk
Open	Daily 9.30–6 Apr–Sep; daily 10–4 Oct–Mar

Castle Acre

Castle Acre was raised by William de Warenne soon after the Conquest and was the principal manor among his properties in Norfolk. Extensive excavations at the site show that the first building was a two-storey manor house reinforced in the mid-12th century to construct a keep. The great tower was never finished, though, and a second phase of refortification, where the keep was reduced in size and the outer defences strengthened, was initiated. In later times, the family moved to accommodation in the lower ward.

The remains

There are visible remains of the west gate: it was probably used by the constable of the castle and seems to have been occupied up to the 14th century although the castle was derelict by 1397. The de Warennes founded a town adjacent to the castle and a Cluniac monastery. The bailey gate is still extant in the village and remains of the monastery are extensive. Substantial earthworks and some stone remain.

Location	Nr Swaffham, Norfolk
Map ref	TF 819152
Tel	0870 333 1181
Web	www.english-heritage.org.uk
Open	Access at all reasonable times

Castle Rising

Castle Rising (pictured opposite) stands on a large site with deep Norman man-made ditches and banks extending to around 4.8ha (12 acres). The oval-shaped inner bailey, sandwiched between two smaller outer baileys, contains the foundations of an 11th-century Norman chapel and the extensive remains of the great 'hall' keep which is dated c.1138–40. There are also ruins of a gatehouse from the same period.

A royal home

Built by William d'Albini II to celebrate his marriage to the widow of Henry I and his consequent acquisition of the Earldom of Sussex, this elegant keep, one of the most important in East Anglia, was one of the most ornate castle/palaces in the country with a noted forebuilding at its east end. For three decades after she was implicated in the murder of Edward II at Berkeley Castle, Castle Rising was the home of Isabella, mother of Edward III. When Isabella died in 1358, the castle passed to her grandson, Edward, the Black Prince. Eventually falling into decline, the site became part of the Howard family estate at the end of the 16th century.

Visiting the castle

The taped audio tour helps visitors to visualize the original castle although the keep is intact. Visitors should note that there are steep steps up to the site and that the car park surface is uneven.

Although there are no refreshments on the site, visitors can bring picnics.

Location	Nr King's Lynn, Norfolk
Map ref	TF 666246
Tel	01553 631330
Web	www.english-heritage.org.uk
Open	Daily 10–6 mid-Mar to Oct; Wed–Sun 10–4 Nov–Mar

Chillingham

A licence to crenellate Chillingham was granted in 1344. What was little more than a single tower built in the previous century became an extensive but compact quadrangular castle with square-angle towers, and a curtain of which there are scant remains.

A haunted castle

Somewhat altered over the centuries and the subject of wide-ranging restoration by its present occupants, Chillingham is, nevertheless, a fine example of a medieval castle with Tudor additions and is still the family home of descendants of the original owners. The castle came under attack in 1536 and suffered some damage during the Pilgrimage of Grace rebellion but was successfully defended. Chillingham has the reputation of being one of the most haunted castles in England.

Restoration and renovation

In the 16th century the main entrance was repositioned in preparation for a visit to the castle by James VI of Scotland; further alterations were carried out in the 18th and 19th centuries. Sir Jeffrey Wyatville, who also worked at Windsor Castle, laid out the grounds.

Rooms and suites in the castle have been renovated to their original splendour. The state rooms have silk-screened walls and there is a restored Elizabethan ceiling in the James I Drawing Room. The Edward I Room is the oldest in the castle and has been re-created to its 13th-century style, with armour and furniture of the time. Paintings of monarchs are displayed in the great hall alongside tapestries, weapons and armour. The dungeons and torture chamber with their ranges of items once used to extract information might frighten younger children.

Location	Northumberland
Map ref	NU 061257
Tel	01668 215359
Web	www.chillingham.castle.com
Open	Easter, Sun–Fri May–Sep. Grounds and tea room 12–5, Castle 1–4.30 (last entry)

Colchester

Colchester – its dimensions a powerful 46 x 33.5m (151 x 110ft) – is one of the first and the largest of the great keeps in Britain built by the Normans.

Roman antecedents

William I ordered a stone castle to be built on the strategic route between East Anglia and London.

The castle was begun in the late 1070s or the 1080s and probably built under the supervision of Gundulf, Bishop of Rochester, the builder of the White Tower at London. Due to a lack of local quality stone the Norman builders plundered Roman Colchester (it had been the first Roman capital of Britain) to build their keep. They chose a site over the ruined Roman Temple of Claudius, the most famous building in Roman Britain, incorporating its base into the foundations of the great tower.

The building plan

Colchester and the White Tower in London were built to much the same plan, both with an apsidal extension although Colchester's corner turrets are more pronounced and its main staircase is the largest diameter newel staircase in Britain measuring 5m (16ft) across. It is thought that the castle had only one floor at first, as it is still possible to see traces of crenellations in the wall. It could be that during construction it was required to be defended at short notice and was hurriedly crenellated, then when the danger had passed, work on the other floors was restarted.

A gruesome history

Colchester saw little action; it was attacked by John in 1216 as it had been taken by the French, but it remained Crown property in the care of a succession of stewards or constables throughout medieval times. By the 13th century Colchester was in use as a prison and at times many hundreds of prisoners of war were confined here in appalling conditions. Much of the castle was a ruin by the 16th century although it continued in use as a county gaol until 1668 and even after that was a prison until 1835. One of the most infamous episodes of this period was when Mathew Hopkins, the Witchfinder General, operated from the castle between 1645 and 1647.

Restoration

At the end of the 17th century the castle was bought by a private owner who wanted to demolish it and then in 1727 was given away as a wedding present to Charles Gray, a lawyer and antiquarian. Gray was responsible for the restoration of Colchester although at the time he believed it to be a Roman construction.

What to see

Today Colchester Castle is the site of an exciting, award-winning museum of Colchester's history, displaying one of the country's finest collections of Roman archaeology and other items recovered from the area. Also on display is Colchester's Royal Charter from 1413. Tour guides have a lively fund of stories to keep visitors amused as they explore.

Location	Essex
Map ref	TL 998254
Tel	Museum: 01206 282939
Web	www.colchestermusuems.org.uk
Open	Mon–Sat 10–5, Sun 11–5. Last admission 30 mins before closing

Clifford's Tower

Williame the Conqueror built two motte castles in York on opposite banks of the River Ouse. Attacked by the Vikings, they were destroyed in 1069 and both were later rebuilt. The motte on the north side of the Ouse supported a timber great tower, but it was burned during the anti-Jewish riots in 1190.

Henry III ordered a rebuild in 1245 and over the next 25 years a curtain with several towers and two gateways was raised round the bailey while the huge motte was adorned with an unusual great tower, now called Clifford's Tower, which has superb views over York, revealing why the site was so important.

The motte on the south side of the river was described in the 14th century as *vetus ballium* (Old Baile) and it is known as Baile Hill.

Location	York, North Yorkshire
Map ref	SE 605515
Tel	01904 646940
Web	www.english-heritage.org.uk
Open	Daily 10–6 mid-Mar to Sep; daily 10–5 Oct; daily 10–4 Nov to mid-Mar

Compton

Dating from the 14th century Compton was built by, and remains, the home of the Gilbert family. Sir Humphrey Gilbert, a half-brother of Sir Walter Raleigh, colonized Newfoundland. The castle was a location in the 1995 film of Jane Austen's *Sense and Sensibility*.

French raids

Compton was fortified against French raids on the south Devon coast. The manor is just 6km (4 miles) from Torquay and hides behind a 6m (20ft) curtain wall.

Of particular interest to visitors and for an insight into the workings of a medieval kitchen is the Great Kitchen with its bread ovens. The grounds include a formal garden, a courtyard garden and a walled garden.

Location	Nr Marldon, Devon
Map ref	SX 865648
Tel	01803 875740 (Answerphone)
Web	www.nationaltrust.org.uk
Open	Apr–Oct Mon, Wed, Thu 10–12.15, 2–5

Conisbrough

Conisbrough Castle was built around 1180–1200 by Hamelin Plantagenet, illegitimate half-brother to Henry II. It stands on the site of an earlier fortress, which was held by William de Warenne and probably built c.1070. Hamelin, the 5th Earl de Warenne, created a great tower castle enclosed in a curtain wall with flanking solid half cylindrical towers and a gatehouse with projecting barbican (of which there are a few remains).

A unique great tower

The principal feature of the castle is the uniquely shaped great tower (unique, that is, in Britain, as there is a similar de Warenne stronghold at Mortemer near Dieppe in France). Constructed from limestone ashlar, the tower is cylindrical with six wedge-shaped buttresses placed equidistantly round the outer wall and is notable for the scarcity of window openings and arrow-loops. It had the disadvantage of most cylindrical towers in that the entrance was not protected by a forebuilding. However, the castle was never put to the test of a siege and Conisbrough remained mostly in the hands of the de Warenne family until the 14th century when it passed to the Crown. It was quite ruinous by the 16th century and this probably saved it from further destruction after the Civil War.

Conisbrough has been made more famous by inspiring Sir Walter Scott to write his epic novel *Ivanhoe*.

For the visitor

The castle offers an interesting day out with plenty to see and regular events. Special tours on some weekends need to be pre-booked. Refreshments are available.

Location	Nr Doncaster, South Yorkshire
Map ref	SK 515989
Tel	01709 863329
Web	www.conisbroughcastle.org.uk
Open	Apr–Sep 10–5; Oct–Mar 10–4

Corfe

The jagged ruins of this once-powerful fortress dominate the horizon at the entrance to the Isle of Purbeck. Corfe Castle was a favourite residence of King John, who built remarkable domestic quarters there, creating the best-appointed apartments of any royal castle in England at the time.

History

Originally a motte castle built in the late 11th century, the outline of Corfe's precincts remained the same for most of its history. The keep probably dates from the reign of Henry I. Henry's brother, Robert, Duke of Normandy, was held at Corfe after his defeat at Tinchebrai in 1106.

The fall of Normandy to the French in 1204 and the castle's location close to the south coast doubtless added momentum to the strengthening of its defences. When King Stephen besieged the castle 60 years earlier, the outer baileys were probably protected only by wooden palisades; a stone curtain and defensive towers (not completed until around 1285) must have been pressing additions. Henry III continued improving the defences at Corfe and spent even more on the castle than King John.

The Civil War

Corfe lost its royal status in the 16th century when Elizabeth I sold it, and was owned by Sir John Bankes by the time the Civil War broke

out in 1642. The garrison at Corfe, led by Sir John's widow after his death in 1644, held out against the Parliamentarians during two sieges but an act of treachery forced capitulation in February 1646. The following month the order came for Corfe to be slighted. This led to the virtual destruction of what must have been one of Britain's most fascinating castles.

Attractions

Visitors today can still see some of the features that survive, including the gloriette. The visitor centre has an interactive exhibition, and events such as living history weekends and Civil War re-enactments help to paint a picture of life in the castle in its heyday. Children will enjoy climbing up to the ruins and exploring the surrounding area. After all this activity a tea room provides welcome refreshments.

Location	Corfe Castle, Dorset
Map ref	SY 959824
Tel	01929 481294
Web	www.nationaltrust.org.uk
Open	Apr–Sep 10–6; Mar & Oct 10–5; Nov–Feb 10–4

The castle today remains much as it was following its Civil War slighting in 1646, after an act of treachery led to its capture by the Parliamentarians.

Dartmouth

The distinctive towers of Dartmouth Castle, one cylindrical and one square, command the cliffs at the narrowest part of the entrance to Devon's Dart Estuary.

A defensive history

A fortress was first built here around 1400 when the town's mayor, John Hawley (said to have been the inspiration for the Shipman of Dartmouth in Chaucer's *Canterbury Tales*), was given a royal order to build a castle to protect the town and river from attack by the French. The corporation received an annual grant of £30 'to repair and keep it garnished with guns'. This sum was increased to £40 by Henry VII in 1486.

Further additions were made during the 15th century when Dartmouth Castle received the first purpose-built artillery tower in the country. More gun emplacements were added to this fortress during its long defensive history, which included a successful siege by Royalist forces, led by Prince Maurice, during the English Civil War (the 500-strong garrison capitulated to the Parliamentarians under Sir Thomas Fairfax after holding the fortress for three years). Dartmouth's last gun emplacements were erected, and manned, during World War II.

For visitors

There are displays in the castle depicting its long history and you can walk along the battlements and see the cannon facing out to sea.

Location	Devon
Map ref	SX 887503
Tel	01803 833588
Web	www.english-heritage.org.uk
Open	Daily 10–5 late Mar–Jun, Sep 10–5; daily 10–6 Jul–Aug; daily 10–4 Oct

Dunstanburgh

Dunstanburgh was a lavish stonework enclosure castle whose main feature was the huge gatehouse tower at the southern end. The first buildings were erected in the early 14th century and included the massive three-storey gatehouse, with its cylindrical towers rising another two storeys. Now in ruins, the gatehouse contained a great hall on the second floor, with tall, mullioned and transomed windows positioned at each end.

A Lancastrian stronghold

Built by Thomas, Earl of Lancaster who opposed Edward II for his bad government and his infelicitous choice of friends (particularly Piers Gaveston), Dunstanburgh passed in due course to John of Gaunt. In the 1370s and 1380s John closed up the entrance to the gatehouse with a stone wall and a forebuilding (now disappeared) and turned it into a residential great tower, building an alternative gateway with barbican. Dunstanburgh, a Lancastrian stronghold, was besieged during the Wars of the Roses and suffered much damage from the Yorkist cannons.

Dunstanburgh is now an impressive ruin standing high on the cliffs above the sea.

Location	Nr Craster, Northumberland
Map ref	NU 258220
Tel	01665 576231 (Custodian)
Web	www.nationaltrust.org.uk
Open	Daily 10–6 Apr–Sep; 1–4 Oct; Thu–Mon 10–4 Nov–Mar

Dunster

The present imposing fortified manor house known as Dunster is a replacement of an earlier Norman earthwork castle built by the de Mohun family. Stonework was later added although there are no remains except for a mound, scarped out of a natural hill.

Owners for six centuries

The Luttrell family bought Dunster in 1376 and lived there for 600 years. Little damage was inflicted during the Civil War even though it was a Parliamentary stronghold, captured by the Royalists and retaken by the Parliamentarians after a long siege. Successive generations of the family have made their mark on the castle, only the 13th-century gatehouse remains of the medieval edifice. Dunster's last restoration was in the 19th century by the Victorian architect Salvin, who reconstructed parts of the manor in Gothic Revival style.

The castle grounds

The grounds shelter subtropical plants and the National Collection of Strawberry Trees while the terraces offer views over Exmoor and the Bristol Channel.

Location	Nr Minehead, Somerset
Map ref	SS 995435
Tel	01643 821314
Web	www.nationaltrust.org.uk
Open	Sat–Wed 11–5 mid-Mar to Oct; early Nov 11–4. Gardens and park: daily, core hours 11–4

Durham

The site of Durham started as a motte castle, erected in a loop of the River Wear granted to the Prince-bishop of Durham in 1072. The chapel of 1080 still survives.

The Bishop's Palace

In the early 12th century a shell enclosure of sandstone in roughly octagonal plan was erected on the motte around the wooden tower and this may have remained for some time; the shell was destroyed in 1340 and rebuilt. Domestic buildings were added within the banked, ditched and partly curtained bailey, including a range to the north, a 13th- to 14th-century great hall, a gatehouse and a kitchen. Although primarily a bishops' palace rather than a fortress, the castle was always kept ready for defence. Prince-bishops were expected to levy an army in times of threat, in return for absolute power over their bishopric.

The University

The keep was rebuilt in the middle of the 19th century when the castle became the site of Durham University but the great hall, used as the dining hall of University College, is medieval. It was first built by Bishop Antony Bek (1284–1311) and then altered by Bishop Thomas Hatfield later in the 14th century. The walls of the palace-castle were connected with the city's walls, and the entire peninsula was enclosed by the river, with the magnificent cathedral included.

Together with the cathedral, the castle at Durham has been declared a UNESCO World Heritage Site.

Location	City of Durham, Co. Durham
Map ref	NZ 273423
Tel	0191 334 3800 (Porter)
Web	www.durhamcastle.com
Open	Daily Easter–Sep, guided tours only

Dover

When William the Conqueror landed at Pevensey with his invading army in September 1066 he quickly pushed on and by November he had reached Dover, leaving garrisoned timber strongholds in his wake. Nothing remains of these fortifications at Dover, and it was more than a century later when Henry II began to rebuild and transform this castle into a powerful medieval stronghold.

A great coastal fortress

Military engineer Maurice (the 'Ingeniator') designed Dover as the first fortress in Western Europe with concentric defences. Henry II also built the massive keep, completed *c.*1190, which continued to be used in a military capacity until the middle of the 20th century. Dover's defences were severely tested when the castle was besieged and undermined by the French in 1216. After this Henry III commissioned the strengthening of the northern defences and these included a unique system of tunnels. He also built accommodation including a great hall. Edward IV modernized the keep in the second half of the 15th century. Although Dover was built primarily for defence it also had to accommodate royalty and VIPs who were travelling overseas. The castle remained in constant use but after the 1500s Dover's defensive importance diminished as artillery power increased.

The Napoleonic threat

The fortress enjoyed a renaissance during the 18th century when its role as a defence against land assaults on Dover and its harbour was increased. New barracks were added and most of the inner bailey's buildings date from then. The growing threat from France during the Napoleonic Wars led to more defences.

Throughout the 19th century the garrison continued to swell and so did its buildings.

Two world wars

Dover remained highly important through both world wars. In May 1940 the operations room beneath the castle was the control centre for Operation Dynamo: the evacuation of Dunkirk, which rescued 338,000 troops. For the rest of World War II, Dover continued as a vital control centre. A garrison was maintained here until the late 1950s. Few castles have maintained such an active role across so many centuries.

The network of tunnels which served as an operations centre in World War II was dug during the Napoleonic Wars and the barracks located there housed up to 2,000 troops. In the 1960s the tunnels were equipped to serve as a base for the government in the event of a nuclear attack on London. Declassified in the 1980s, they are a highlight of a visit here.

A lot of attractions

However, there is much more to do and see: The Princess of Wales Royal Regiment Museum, the Roman Pharos and a Saxon church. Exhibitions demonstrate the strategic importance of the castle during its long history. There is also a restaurant and a café.

Location	Kent
Map ref	TR 325419
Tel	01304 211067
Web	www.english-heritage.org.uk
Open	Daily 10–6 late Mar–Jun & Sep; 9.30–6.40 Jul–Aug; 10–5 Oct; Thu–Mon 1–4 Nov–Jan; 10–4 Feb–Mar

Farleigh Hungerford

The manor house at Farleigh, sited with its back to a deep dyke, was built by the Montfort family and sold to the first Speaker of the House of Commons, Sir Thomas Hungerford, in 1369. Following the custom of the time, Sir Thomas fortified the house and built a square enclosure with curtain, cylindrical corner towers and an extensive array of domestic buildings. He failed to obtain a licence to crenellate but received a pardon for this oversight in 1383. Walter, Sir Thomas' son, added an outer bailey and moat to Farleigh Hungerford in the 15th century. The church of St Leonard, notable for its 14th-century wall paintings and the Hungerford tombs, was within its precincts and used as the castle chapel.

Falling into decay, stone from the castle was eventually used to build nearby Farleigh House. Farleigh Hungerford's extensive remains are still impressive and there is an interesting museum on site. Occasional events take place in the summer.

Location	Nr Trowbridge, Somerset
Map ref	ST 801576
Tel	01225 754026
Web	www.english-heritage.org.uk
Open	Daily 10–5 late Mar–Jun & Sep; 10–6 Jul–Aug; Sat–Sun 10–4 Oct–Mar

Framlingham

Framlingham Castle (pictured below) was built between 1189 and 1200 by Roger Bigod, the Earl of Norfolk, on the site of an earlier castle destroyed on the orders of Henry II in 1175.

History

The castle was besieged in 1216 and taken on behalf of King John, but as there is no evidence of major siege damage, it is likely that the defenders gave in without much of a fight. A great hall, built by the Bigods, was pulled down in the 17th century and has disappeared into the masonry of a poorhouse.

In 1553 Mary Tudor learned she was the Queen of England after her younger brother Edward VI had died while she was staying at Framlingham.

For the visitor

The audio tour is very informative. A variety of events for all age groups take place here throughout the year, including plays, and displays of birds of prey.

Location	Suffolk
Map ref	TM 287637
Tel	01728 724189
Web	www.english-heritage.org.uk
Open	Daily 10–6 late Mar–Sep; 10–5 Oct; 10–4 Nov–Mar

Goodrich

The castle is set on a high rocky spur over the right bank of the River Wye, commanding a crossing of the river. It is protected partly by a natural steep slope and valley and partly by a moat cut out of the rock. By 1102, it was known as Godric's Castle, after Godric the first lord here.

A formidable fortress

A square great tower was the first stone building at Goodrich in the middle of the 12th century. The tower stood alone for a time, then late in the 13th century, when Goodrich was held by the de Valence family, the fortress was substantially renovated. It was converted into a formidable quadrangle with massive cylindrical towers on three corners, and a vast gatehouse tower on the fourth (northeast) corner. The cylindrical towers were raised on square bases with spurs that clamped the towers to their rock bases. Elaborate apartments were built inside the quadrangle, including a great hall, a solar and kitchens. The northeast corner tower was built as a gatehouse that included a chapel.

The Civil War

Goodrich was held for Parliament at the start of the Civil War and garrisoned with 100 men. The Royalists then held it for a time and the castle was partly demolished.

A satisfying place to explore, Goodrich is perfect for wandering around and will appeal to castle-lovers and children alike.

Location	Nr Ross-on-Wye, Herefordshire
Map ref	SO 577200
Tel	01600 890538
Web	www.english-heritage.org.uk
Open	Daily 10–5 Mar–May, Sep–Oct; 10–6 Jun–Aug; Thu–Mon 10–4 Nov–Feb

Hedingham

A place of superlatives, Hedingham's great tower is one of the most famous Norman keeps in the country. In 1140, Aubrey de Vere II built the tower on the site of an earlier timber fortress. The tower today stands at over 33m (110ft), its walls filled at every storey with chambers and passages. Considered one of the finest Norman domestic interiors still existing, the banqueting hall is spanned by a vast Norman arch.

The de Vere family

The de Veres were an important family from the time of the Conquest, and favourites in the Tudor court. Aubrey de Vere III was created 1st Earl of Oxford by Queen Matilda and a later de Vere was one of the barons who compelled King John to consent to the Magna Carta. There were many later alterations to the castle buildings but only the Norman great tower remains.

In the 18th century Hedingham was sold to Sir William Ashurst, Lord Mayor of London, who built a large country house in the grounds. The estate later passed into the possession of descendants of the de Vere family, through marriage.

The castle grounds

Visit this castle for its wonderful grounds as much as for the castle itself. Visitors can enjoy lakeside walks and trails through the woodlands. In the summer there are many events (telephone or visit the website for details) including jousting and living history displays. A tea room provides refreshments.

Location	Castle Hedingham, Essex
Map ref	TL 787359
Tel	01787 460261
Web	www.hedinghamcastle.co.uk
Open	Sun–Thu 10–5 mid-Apr to Sep. Check website for closures

Helmsley

The most striking thing about this stone enclosure castle of the late 12th to early 13th century is the huge earthwork ditch-and-bank defences. Built as a quadrangle inside another quadrangle, the castle was well defended: the ditches are over 9m (30ft) deep. These earthworks are related to an earlier castle built in the first half of the 12th century.

A defensive castle

Robert de Roos rebuilt the castle in stone and erected a thick curtain wall with D-end and round flanking towers along the edge of the platform in the inner quadrangle. On the northeast of the wall he added a rectangular great tower and another great tower in the west, which remains. The Lordship of Helmsley stayed with the de Roos name until 1478.

A family home

The Manners family inherited the lordship and created a fashionable Elizabethan residence. Helmsley was not attacked until the Civil War when it was besieged by Parliamentarians: this peaceful affair ended when the defenders surrendered through lack of food. Sir Thomas Fairfax dismantled most of the fortress but kept the Elizabethan west range intact.

Attractions for the visitor

The visitor centre displays objects retrieved from the site, including unusual arrows that show Helmsley was at the centre of weapon technology. Interactive displays further demonstrate the importance of the castle and living history events are staged.

Location	North Yorkshire
Map ref	SE 611836
Tel	01439 770442
Web	www.english-heritage.org.uk
Open	Daily 10–6 Apr–Sep; Thu–Mon 10–4 Oct–Mar

Hever

An enchanting, fortified manor house with a massive gatehouse, walled bailey and double moat, Hever was begun in the 1270s: a licence to refortify it was granted in 1340 to William de Hever.

Anne Boleyn

In c.1460 Geoffrey Bullen, Lord Mayor of London and great-grandfather to Anne Boleyn, acquired Hever. It was greatly modified by the Bullens who created a comfortable Tudor home in which Anne, the second wife of Henry VIII and mother of Elizabeth I, spent her youth. After Anne's execution and on the death of her father, Henry VIII passed the castle to Anne of Cleves as part of their divorce settlement.

Home to the Astors

In 1903 its new owner, statesman and financier William Waldorf Astor lavished money on the by now neglected buildings and restored Hever to its former glory: he added a number of Tudor-style houses nearby to form a 'village', and the magnificent gardens. The work included digging out the 14ha (35 acre) lake. The Italian Garden is the setting for a collection of classical statuary.

Wonderful visitors' attractions

Hever is a wonderful place to visit. There is an adventure playground for children, and two mazes. In the gardens is a collection of miniature houses (1:12 scale) showing life from the 11th to the early 20th centuries. The castle houses a wealth of portraits, tapestries and furniture. Two Books of Hours inscribed by Anne Boleyn are on display. Arms and armour and costumed figures add even more interest to the interior. Restaurants provide visitors with refreshments.

Location	Nr Edenbridge, Kent
Map ref	TQ 478452
Tel	01732 865224
Web	www.hevercastle.co.uk
Open	Castle daily 12–6 Mar–Oct, gardens open at 11; 12–5 Nov

Leeds

eeds Castle's origins date to Saxon times when the manor was known as Esledes. Robert de Crevecoeur built a stone castle here in 1119, on a site near an earlier fortified mill.

Royal ownership

The castle was handed to Edward I and his wife Eleanor of Castile at the end of the 13th century and remained in royal ownership (although not entirely unbroken) for the next 300 years. Edward and his queen made many improvements, both defensive and domestic:

the first building, the keep (or gloriette as it is called here), stands on its own small island. Other buildings were erected on the main island and the two were connected originally by drawbridge and later bridged with a corridor.

Castle of the queens

After Eleanor died, Edward granted Leeds to his new queen, Margaret. From then on Leeds Castle was often given to the Queens of England as a part of their dower. Edward III continued work on the castle but it was

Henry VIII, when he married his first wife, Catherine of Aragon, who transformed it into a magnificent palace. The end of Henry's reign was to mark the end of the royal ownership of Leeds Castle as Edward VI's Protectors granted it to St Anthony St Leger (Sheriff of Kent) and it then passed through various interconnecting families, some of whom carried out alterations and modifications to the castle.

20th-century transformation

The 19th-century work by Wykeham Martin left Leeds' exterior largely as it stands today (Wykeham built the Tudor-style New Castle which was completed in 1823) then in the 1920s a wealthy Anglo-American, Lady Baillie (as she was to become) bought the castle and transformed its interior with the help of the French designers Rateau and Boudin. It is Lady Baillie's legacy, the result of a life's work and passion, on show at Leeds Castle today.

Leeds Castle is regarded as one of the world's most beautiful palaces. The castle, owned by six queens, and one of Henry VIII's favourite residences, has been developed across 900 years. A vibrant social powerhouse from the 1930s, its owner Lady Baillie established its reputation as one of the 20th century's great houses, where foreign royalty and leading figures in politics and entertainment were magnificently entertained. Lady Baillie died in 1974 but the castle continues as a meeting place for history makers: as well as a popular visitor attraction the castle is a top-level conference venue.

For the visitor

You can spend a day visiting the castle, whose grounds extend to 220ha (500 acres) and include formal gardens, an aviary, a maze with an underground grotto, twice-daily falconry displays and a museum dedicated to dog collars. Inside the castle you can see rooms that reflect Leeds Castle's history, from Henry VIII's Banqueting Hall to Lady Baillie's drawing room with their rich furnishings and decorations. Audio tours will fill in the blanks and in the rooms guides can help with further information. For refreshments there is the choice of a restaurant or a tea room.

Location	Maidstone, Kent
Map ref	TQ 836533
Tel	01622 765400
Web	www.leeds-castle.com
Open	Grounds daily 10–7 Apr–Oct. Daily 10–5 Nov–Mar

Kenilworth

This is one of the grandest ruined castles in England. Henry I granted Kenilworth to his chamberlain, Geoffrey de Clinton in 1120, and later in the century a substantial great tower and a stone curtain were built.

A dramatic history

The castle was favoured by royalty and enhanced by various royal patrons, but in 1253 Henry III passed Kenilworth to the de Montforts under a lifetime grant. The siege at Kenilworth, between Simon de Montfort's supporters and Prince Edward's army, was a major incident of the Barons' War. John of Gaunt added palatial buildings and in the 16th century, when the castle was home to Robert Dudley, Earl of Leicester, and a favourite of Queen Elizabeth I, Kenilworth was further embellished. Elizabeth was a frequent visitor to the castle during this time and was lavishly entertained on her visits.

The castle changed hands twice during the Civil War and was slighted, but only minimally. It was after this that the ingenious and magnificent great moat/lake, created by damming the streams flowing through the marshy land below the castle, was lost. Such was the impact of this grand castle that, in 1821, Sir Walter Scott wrote a two-volume novel about Elizabeth and Dudley named after it.

Visiting

The Tudor gardens are well worth strolling through and the audio tour is the best way to appreciate the history built into the fabric of this castle. There is a tea room for refreshments.

Location	Warwickshire
Map ref	SP 278723
Tel	01926 852078
Web	www.english-heritage.org.uk
Open	Daily 10—5 Mar–May, Sep–Oct; 10–6 Jun–Aug; 10–4 Nov–Feb

Lewes

Lewes, one of the few castles with two mottes associated with one bailey (see Lincoln, opposite), was raised with defensive earthworks and a dry moat in 1069–70, by William de Warenne, later Earl of Surrey. At the time the River Ouse was navigable, and Lewes was a useful port and important river crossing, and Warenne made the site his main seat and headquarters. He was buried in Lewes Priory, along with his wife Gundrada.

The barbican

The first wooden castle here was probably built on the northeastern Brack Mount, but defensive priorities shifted so the 12th-century shell keep, with its 13th-century octagonal towers and the 14th-century barbican are on or near the westerly mound. Parts of the bailey wall and the Norman gatehouse remain. The barbican is one of the finest in the country – built of knapped flint, it has corbelled round towers on the corners and a machicolated parapet over the centre pointed arch. From the top there are magnificent views over the site of the Battle of Lewes, fought in May 1264, when Simon de Montfort and the barons defeated Henry III and occupied the town.

The decline

Lewes Castle declined in importance from the 15th century and over the following years became little more than an admirable ruin. Barbican House next to the castle houses a museum with a sound and light show telling the story of the town.

Location	East Sussex
Map ref	TQ 415101
Tel	01273 486260
Web	www.sussexpast.co.uk/lewescastle
Open	Tue–Sat 10–5.30 (closed Mon in Jan), Sun 11–5.30

Lincoln

Lincoln Castle is built on a site of a Roman fort and like Lewes it has two mottes associated with one bailey. It was started in 1068 on the orders of William the Conqueror and 166 Saxon houses were cleared to enlarge the site and allow the castle with its earthworks to be erected.

The two mottes

The western motte is topped with an interesting 12th-century shell keep known as the Lucy Tower. Ranulf, Earl of Chester, held the castle in the 1140s and was granted leave to refortify it by King Stephen: the name Lucy stems from Ranulf's mother, Lucy, Countess of Chester, who died c.1136, passing the castle to her son. The second motte carries a square-plan tower with a 19th-century observatory. The immense 12th-century curtain remains in excellent preservation, the wall-walks give good views of the castle site and surrounding town and countryside.

Lincoln was besieged during the Barons' War in the 13th century but its main use has been as a court and a prison; many prisoners were executed on the ramparts and buried in the castle precincts.

Walks and attractions

There are wall walks and a heraldry centre at the castle as well as dungeons. One of the four remaining original copies of the Magna Carta is on display at the castle. Guides take you through the castle at 11 and 2 each day and their extensive knowledge and stories will enhance your visit. A café is on the site.

The Lucy Tower (above) a shell enclosure with wing walls is one of the main surviving buildings of Lincoln Castle.

Location	Lincolnshire
Map ref	SK 974718
Tel	01522 511068
Web	www.lincolnshire.gov.uk
Open	Mon–Sat 9.30–5.30, Sun 11–5.30

Ludlow

Described by Daniel Defoe in 1722 as 'the very perfection of decay', Ludlow Castle was begun by the de Lacys in the 11th century, one of a string of fortresses along the borderlands between England and the yet unconquered Welsh territories. Some of the earliest surviving parts of the castle are remnants of their work, including the unusual gatehouse/keep and a Norman chapel in the inner bailey. Among the earliest castle chapels to be built in Britain, its circular nave is still standing. Round chapels were associated with the Knights Templar.

Roger Mortimer

The de Lacys held Ludlow until the end of the 13th century when the castle came into the possession of the de Genevilles and then at the beginning of the 14th century, the infamous Roger Mortimer. Mortimer's Tower, which stands out at the castle for its semicircular design, takes its name from its treacherous occupant but was, in fact, built by the de Genevilles. Roger Mortimer did build the Chapel of St Peter, to celebrate his escape from the Tower of London. Mortimer was imprisoned after he and his lover Queen Isabella were implicated in the murder of Edward II. Eventually becoming too powerful, Roger Mortimer was arrested at Nottingham and put to death in 1330.

Two royal dramas

In 1461 Ludlow began more than three centuries of royal ownership and the castle gradually became the centre of administration for the Marches and for Wales. Edward IV's son was sent to live here and a Prince's Council was formed from members of his household. Prince Edward was at Ludlow when his father died. The new king and his brother travelled to London but were imprisoned in the Tower of

London by their uncle, the Duke of Gloucester. Edward and his brother disappeared and their uncle was crowned King Richard III. The story of the princes has become one of the Tower's most famous legends, and even today their fate remains uncertain.

Ludlow also had a cameo role in the years leading up to the Reformation as Henry Tudor's eldest son Prince Arthur died here in 1502. Arthur's wife, Catherine of Aragon, was to become the first wife of Arthur's brother, Henry VIII; it was the separation of this union that led to one of the most momentous periods of British history.

A seat of government

The last few decades of the 16th century saw a period of massive building work. Ludlow wasn't just a royal residence, but a regional government office, court and prison. Both the town and castle were besieged by the Parliamentarians during the Civil War when its loyalties lay with the Royalists, but the castle suffered little damage. Its demise came later in the century when government control was centralized in London and Ludlow was abandoned.

Fun attractions

A range of events, including special half-term and summer holiday festivities, provide plenty of fun for all visitors. The substantial ruins are satisfying to explore, and you can take a walk around the walls of the outer bailey.

Location	Shropshire
Map ref	SO 508746
Tel	01584 873355
Web	www.ludlowcastle.com
Open	Sat–Sun 10–4 Jan; daily 10–4 Feb–Mar & Oct–Dec; 10–5 Apr–Jul & Sep; 10–7 Aug

Lydford

This is an example of a castle whose great tower was raised before the motte, which was then piled up around the tower base. Measuring around 16m (52ft) square, the late 12th-century tower is now roofless. It was repaired in the 18th century and used as a gaol and stannary (tin-mining) court, but fell into decay again.

Location	Nr Okehampton, Devon
Map ref	SX 509848
Tel	0870 333 1181
Web	www.english-heritage.org.uk
Open	At any reasonable time

Middleham

A motte castle was built at Middleham but the motte was abandoned and is known today as William's Hill. In *c*.1170, Robert FitzRanulph was granted leave to build a great tower on a site southwest of the motte and a surprisingly substantial structure with palatial accommodation emerged. In the 13th century, the magnificent great tower was enclosed in a quadrangular curtain with buildings ranged along three sides, including corner towers and gatehouse, and yet more buildings were added in the 14th and 15th centuries. The castle was also surrounded by a moat.

Royal history

Middleham came into the possession of the Nevilles, passing eventually to the Earl of Warwick, and for ten years before his death in 1471 the castle was a political and social powerhouse. Warwick's daughter married the Duke of Gloucester, who later became Richard III, and their only son was born here and then died at age ten. Henry VII seized Middleham after Richard's death and it remained a royal castle until very early in the 17th century but no royal visits are recorded. Although it was garrisoned during the Civil War, Middleham was never besieged. Nevertheless the castle was ruinous by the 19th century although the extensive remains imply its former grandeur.

Location	Nr Leyburn, North Yorkshire
Map ref	SE 127876
Tel	01969 623899
Web	www.english-heritage.org.uk
Open	Daily 10–6 Apr–Sep; Thu–Mon 10–4 Oct–Mar

LIFE IN EARLY CASTLES

THE FIRST NORMAN CASTLES IN BRITAIN WERE OF WOOD, TYPICALLY ON TOP OF AN ARTIFICIAL MOUND SURROUNDED BY A DITCH AND PALISADE. THESE MOTTE (THE MOUND AND ITS BUILDING) AND BAILEY (THE ENCLOSURE) CASTLES WERE BUILT IN THEIR HUNDREDS ALL OVER ENGLAND AND WALES. MANY CAN STILL BE SEEN AS OVERGROWN MOUNDS WITH NO TRACE OF ANY IDENTIFIABLE BUILDINGS.

These early castles were essential for the invading Normans. They were where they kept their armouries and treasuries, where they retreated to at time of need or for rest, and they were the base from where they controlled their surrounding lands. Many of these early castles were small, and could be built very fast, often making use of the terrain by building the motte on a natural hillock or other features in the landscape, including pre-historic man-made mounds.

Essentially offensive and defensive structures, castles were also where the Norman lords and their families lived. It is this dual role of home and fortress that sets castles apart from all other buildings. The lord knew that he had to make his castle as impregnable as possible, but he also had to live there, and he wanted a degree of comfort, not just for its own sake but to show that he had wealth, power and status. In other words, most lords did not want to be thought of as violent aggressors lurking behind dark defences only to emerge for conflict.

But the fact is that the earliest castles would have been cheerless by our standards: chill, damp and with few furnishings. The two best places to be were the lord's own chamber, where the best furnishings and fittings would be found, and the hall, where everyone ate and where many would sleep, because here fires were kept for cooking and for warmth.

As the Normans consolidated their conquest, so they became richer and could begin to replace their wooden castles with castles of stone. These were more secure (wood was comparitively easy to burn down) and could be more comfortable, with better and bigger ranges of rooms.

Mountfitchet

Robert, Duke of Boulogne, founded this enclosure fortress with bailey, surrounded with extensive ditching and ramparts. A small tower was raised and stone fragments suggest there were additional buildings. Richard Montfitchet II was one of the barons who tried to enforce the Magna Carta. The castle was dismantled by King John in *c*.1215.

A modern reconstruction

The site has been impressively reconstructed as an 11th-century motte and bailey timber castle and Norman village where visitors can wander into buildings to see what life was like in a Norman village. You will also mingle with the domestic animals that roam through the village. The visitor centre displays objects found during excavations, ranging from Roman coins to Civil War weapons. Wax figures in Norman costumes people the rooms and bring them to life. A tea room is open for refreshments.

Location	Stansted Mountfichet, Essex
Map ref	TL 516249
Tel	01279 813237
Web	www.mountfitchet.com
Open	Daily 10–5 mid-Mar to mid-Nov

Muncaster

The castle dominates a strategic site overlooking Scafell Pike. The medieval core of the present building is a pele tower, thought to date from around 1300, built on Roman foundations. Anthony Salvin remodelled and extended the castle in the 1860s.

The 'Luck of Muncaster'

Muncaster has been in the possession of the Pennington family since at least 1208. Legend has it that when Sir John Pennington gave shelter to Henry VI after the Battle of Hexham in 1464, Henry left his drinking bowl at the castle prophesying that as long as it remained 'whole and unbroken' the Pennington family would continue to live and thrive at Muncaster. Today the bowl is still intact, and known as the 'Luck of Muncaster'.

Indoor and outdoor attractions

Still a family home, the castle has large collections of furniture, paintings and cultural artefacts gathered by the Pennington family. Walkers and gardeners will enjoy the wild locations, famous for its views and collections of flowering shrubs. Nearly 10km (6 miles) of paths and trails weave their way through and around the woodland gardens (suitable footwear is recommended).

The World Owl Centre, in the gardens, is home to many species of these creatures and other birds of prey. A talk and displays (when the birds usually fly) takes place daily from February to November. 'Darkest Muncaster' is when the castle and gardens are lit most winter weekend evenings (except January).

Location	Nr Ravenglass, Cumbria
Map ref	SD 103964
Tel	01229 717614
Web	www.muncaster.co.uk
Open	Castle Sun–Fri 12–5 mid-Feb to early Nov. Gardens, Owl Centre daily 10.30–6 (or dusk if earlier) Feb–Dec

Newcastle upon Tyne

Newcastle began as a motte castle with a bank and ditch, built by Robert Curthose, William the Conqueror's eldest son, in 1080. During the late 11th and early 12th centuries ownership of the northern counties of England was disputed with Scotland and for a time Newcastle was held by the Scottish kings.

The great tower

A new, stone castle was begun by Henry II in 1168. Work continued for about ten years under Mauricius Caementarius (Maurice the Engineer), and included a substantial rectangular great tower within a curtain wall. The great tower with its vaulted basement was restored in the mid-19th century and now houses a museum. It is one of the best surviving examples of a Norman keep in the country.

History

The curtain enclosure was many sided, with postern gates and rectangular flanking towers. Additional buildings raised against the inside in later years include the aisled great hall of c.1210 which was dismantled in 1809. In 1247–50 a tower gatehouse, the Black Gate, which survives, was added to the more vulnerable western edge of the castle site. Once the town walls were completed in the middle of the 14th century the castle's defensive significance declined. It was garrisoned again briefly during the Civil War.

Visiting the castle

Visitors can climb a spiral staircase to the restored battlements for good views. The keep and Black Gate are both open and have many areas of interest. The website is excellent.

Location	Tyne and Wear
Map ref	NZ 250638
Tel	0191 2327938
Web	http://museums.ncl.ac.uk/keep/
Open	Daily 9.30–5.30 Apr–Sep; 9.30–4.30 Oct–Mar

Norwich

Norwich castle was raised shortly after the Conquest, at the expense of William I. A large stone keep was added during the reign of Henry I *c.*1125–35. Possibly due to its status as a royal palace, unusually the outside walls were decorated with arcading.

A gaol and a museum

By 1345 the keep was in use as the county gaol, and it remained a prison until 1887 when it was converted into a museum and art gallery. Architect Anthony Salvin carried out a faithful restoration on the tower's exterior in the 1830s when Bath stone was used to replace the original and decaying Caen blocks.

Displays and tours

Norwich Castle Museum is housed in the keep. Apart from the archaeology, art and history displays in the museum, there are tours of the dungeons and battlements with views across Norwich. Displays also give an insight into life in the castle. A café is open for visitors.

Location	Norfolk
Map ref	TG 232085
Tel	01603 493625
Web	www.museums.norfolk.gov.uk
Open	Mon–Fri 10–4.30, Sat 10–5, Sun 1–5

Nunney

A distinctive quadrangular castle with closely spaced circular corner towers and surrounded by a deep moat, the compact French-style Nunney Castle was built by John de la Mere who obtained a licence to crenellate in 1373. It would have been roofed like a French château.

The Civil War

Besieged by the Parliamentarians in 1645 the north wall of the castle was badly damaged by cannon fire: the wall finally collapsed, but not until 1910 when it blocked the moat (since cleared). After the Civil War the castle was slighted and rendered uninhabitable, but it was not destroyed. As a consequence this four-storey fortification with its towers, still almost at their original height, is a substantial ruin, surrounded by one of the deepest moats in England, and makes a dramatic backdrop to the centre of this pretty Somerset village.

Location	Nr Frome, Somerset
Map ref	ST 737457
Tel	0870 333 1181
Web	www.english-heritage.org.uk
Open	Access at reasonable times

Old Sarum

Outlines of foundations and extensive earthworks remain at Old Sarum, an important operational base and royal residence during William I's reign, and the site where he chose to pay off his army in 1070, and take the Oath of Allegiance from his lords in 1086.

An ancient history

Old Sarum has a history dating back to Neolithic times. It was an Iron Age hill fort, the Romans occupied it and it was also a Saxon burh. William the Conqueror put up a motte and bailey castle, then after the Bishopric of Sherborne was transferred to Old Sarum, a cathedral and ecclesiastical buildings were erected inside the bailey. Friction between the inhabitants of the castle and the cathedral led to the move of the episcopal see to a site nearer the river, known as New Sarum, or Salisbury, in the 13th century where a new cathedral was begun in 1220. The castle at Old Sarum received further 12th- and 13th-century additions and remained in use until it was demolished in the early 16th century.

Visiting the site

Today visitors will see much of the earthworks, foundations and fragments of buildings, inlcuding a good stretch of splayed plinth of the postern tower. Many relics that were recovered are now in the Salisbury and Wiltshire Museum in Salisbury itself, 3km (2 miles) from the site. New panels will guide you through Old Sarum's long history.

The English Heritage shop sells refreshments and picnics are permitted on the site. English Heritage arranges events throughout the year, including displays by costumed performers.

Location	Nr Salisbury, Wiltshire
Map ref	SU 138327
Tel	01722 334956 (local tourist information)
Web	www.english-heritage.org.uk
Open	Daily 9–6 Jul–Aug; 10–5 Apr–Jun & Sep; 10–4 Oct & Mar; 11–3 Nov–Feb

Old Wardour

A unique castle driven by design rather than defensive necessity, Old Wardour was built by the 5th Lord Lovel, who obtained a licence to crenellate his home in the 1390s.

A romantic ruin

The Lovels lost Old Wardour after a short time and the Arundell family acquired it. Captured by Parliamentarian forces in 1643 it was reclaimed by Lord Arundell in 1644, but the damage was so severe that the Arundells had to abandon it. They later built a grand mansion in the grounds, keeping the shell as a feature of the parkland. It is one of the country's most romantic ruins with a lakeside setting; scenes from *Robin Hood: Prince of Thieves* were filmed here.

Location	Wardour Park, nr Tisbury, Wiltshire
Map ref	ST 939263
Tel	01747 870487
Web	www.english-heritage.org.uk
Open	Daily 10–5 late Mar–Jun & Sep; 10–6 Jul–Aug; 10–4 Oct; Sat–Sun 10–4 Nov–Mar

Pendennis

O ne of Henry VIII's artillery forts, Pendennis, along with St Mawes, was intended to defend the Fal estuary. Additions to the defences were made during Elizabeth I's reign but the castle was not actually attacked until the Civil War. A Royalist stronghold, Pendennis was besieged from both land and sea.

Location	Nr Falmouth, Cornwall
Map ref	SW 824318
Tel	01326 316594
Web	www.english-heritage.org.uk
Open	Daily 10–5 Apr–Jun & Sep; 10–6 Jul–Aug; 10–4 Oct–Mar. Closes at 4 Sat Apr–Sep

Pevensey

T he Romans built one of their coastal forts on the Saxon shore at Pevensey early in the 4th century AD. Called Anderita (or Anderida), it was an elliptical enclosure with flanking D-ended bastions and is one of the largest surviving such examples in Britain.

The Norman invasion

William the Conqueror landed here with his invading force in September 1066 and they sheltered inside the remains of this fortress. Once the South East of England was under his control, William granted Pevensey to

Location	East Sussex
Map ref	TQ 645048
Tel	01323 762604
Web	www.english-heritage.org.uk
Open	Daily 10–6 Apr–Sep; Sat–Sun 10–4 Oct–Mar

Robert, Count of Mortain, who raised a castle in the east end of the fort using a section of the original Roman curtain wall: the remainder of the Roman enclosure became the outer bailey. An unusual great tower was constructed in c 1100 but this is in ruins.

An observation post

Undergoing periods of development over the next 300 years, Pevensey fell into disrepair by the beginning of the 16th century. The receding coast meant that the shoreline castle was now inland and much of its importance was lost. It was re-armed during the threat of invasion by the Spanish in the late 16th century and, although decaying, used as an observation and command post in World War II. Pillboxes and gun emplacements remain at the castle.

There are extensive views from the wall. The audio tour is included in the entry fee and events are staged in the summer. A tea room serves refreshments.

Peveril

Sometimes known as Castle Peak, Peveril is a very early example of castle building. Raised on a natural, easily defendable and almost inaccessible ridge with two precipitous sides, the first building was a stone curtain, which contained herringbone masonry, along the north side of a triangle; it was continued along other sides in the 12th century. After the revolt of his son Prince Henry, Henry II fortified the castle by adding a 18.5m (60ft) square great tower in 1176. The tower was a simple structure and not really intended to be residential: it was faced with ashlar and cost a little under £200.

Royal ownership

The castle is named after its original owners, the Peverel family. William Peverel forfeited it to Henry II in 1155 after he was disgraced, it is said, for having been involved in the murder of the Earl of Chester. The king took a liking to the site, and the great tower was perhaps intended to be a kind of pied-à-terre. By 1400 the castle's importance had diminished and the keep was used as a courthouse and prison. By the 19th century the castle was ruinous.

Visitors

Extensive renovation works have been carried out and visitors can now access two chambers that had previously been closed. There is a spiral stairway to the base of the keep.

The setting of the castle, on a hill above the town of Castleton, is magnificent with views ranging across the Peak District.

Location	Castleton, Derbyshire
Map ref	SK 149826
Tel	01433 620613
Web	www.english-heritage.org.uk
Open	Daily 10–5 Apr & Sep–Oct; 10–6 May–Aug; Thu–Mon 10–4 Nov–Mar

KINGS, BARONS AND SOCIETY

THE MONARCH WAS AT THE PINNACLE OF MEDIEVAL SOCIETY. HIS RULE WAS ABSOLUTE, BUT HE COULD ONLY RULE WITH THE ACTIVE HELP OF LORDS AND BARONS. THE BARONS THEMSELVES WERE OFTEN IMMENSELY POWERFUL, ESSENTIALLY RULING THE LANDS THEY CONTROLLED. SOMETIMES THEY WORKED TOGETHER FOR THE GOOD OF THE COUNTRY, BUT THERE WERE TIMES WHEN THE BARONS SEEMED THE CREATORS OF ANARCHY AND MISERY.

Feudal society was pyramidal: at the top was the monarch, next came the barons, who were given land by the king in return for loyalty and help in times of strife and war. Next were the knights, who were given land by the barons in return for service. At the bottom were the peasants, or villeins, who did all the manual work. Villeins had few rights and they were sometimes little better than slaves. But society would have collapsed without their work, and the lords knew that.

Later in the Middle Ages, society gradually moved from a service-based structure to one based on money. A new class arose called freemen who were better off than villeins, and were the skilled workers and tradesmen.

The fortunes of the times depended very much on individual monarchs. If they were strong they could hold society together; if weak, then things could unravel very quickly. An example of this is the reign of King Stephen from 1135 to 1154. Stephen was the nephew of the previous king, Henry I, and was crowned by barons who did not like the idea of Henry's rightful heir – Matilda – coming to the throne. Matilda did not accept this, and the ensuing civil war lasted for most of Stephen's reign. Each side courted the barons, who took advantage of the situation.

Castles were central in this struggle. A contemporary account describes the misery created: 'when the castles were built they filled them with devils and wicked men … At regular intervals they levied a tax known as protection money on the villages. When the wretched people had no more to give they plundered and burned all the villages …'

In the reign of King John (1199–1216), the barons showed themselves in a better light, through their insistence on the drawing up of Magna Carta. Although it worked to the advantage of the barons, it put in writing some of the basic tenets of society, and formed the foundation for England's unwritten constitution.

Pickering

This was a motte castle built soon after the Conquest, during William I's northern campaign. The motte was surrounded by a ditch with two baileys enclosing it, in two curved halves. Stone was added between 1180 and 1236. A stone curtain was built and c.1218–36 work was done on constructing a circular shell keep on top of the motte, which was replaced in the 13th century. Various buildings were raised in the two baileys, including a new hall of c.1314, a chapel of c.1227 and the constable's lodgings.

Edward II

Pickering was besieged in the Magna Carta war of 1215–16. Edward II was fond of the castle and lavished nearly £1,000 on it in 1323–6, including replacing the timber palisade around the outer bailey with stone. This outer curtain had three towers, one of which was a prison.

Visitors' attractions

By the 17th century the chapel was the only usable building; today it serves as an exhibition space. Much of the keep, towers and walls remain as substantial ruins. Refreshments are available on site.

Location	North Yorkshire
Map ref	SE 799845
Tel	01751 474989
Web	www.english-heritage.org.uk
Open	Daily 10–6 Apr–Sep; Thu–Mon 10–4 Oct

Pontefract

Pontefract was for a long time the main royal castle in northern England. Used as a residence, arsenal, court and prison, its end came after it was besieged three times during the Civil War and then severely slighted.

The Duchy of Lancaster

Originally a de Lacy holding, Pontefract began as a motte castle of c.1086. Over the next two centuries it acquired two more baileys, and all three received buildings and walls. Through marriage, the castle came to Thomas Plantagenet, Earl of Lancaster and he made extensive additions, but in 1322 Thomas was beheaded for treason at the castle: his lands were eventually restored to his heirs and Pontefract still remains a part of the Duchy of Lancaster. At the end of the 14th century Richard II was imprisoned and died here after Henry Bolingbroke forced his abdication and the House of Lancaster came to the throne.

A significant stronghold

Unsurprisingly the castle was an important Lancastrian stronghold during the Wars of the Roses. However, its significance declined somewhat during Tudor times. Nevertheless it was an important arsenal after the Pilgrimage of Grace in 1536. Major repairs and renovations were made early in the 17th century prior to the Civil War, and when it fell in 1649, the fortress was the last Royalist stronghold to surrender.

The ruins and the cellars under the great hall can be visited. The cellars, down very steep steps, were used as a military store and prison.

Location	West Yorkshire
Map ref	SE 460224
Tel	01977 723440
Web	www.wakefield.gov.uk
Open	Mon–Fri 8.30–dusk, Sat–Sun 10.30–dusk

Portchester

Another Norman castle (see also Pevensey) built within the confines of a late 3rd-century Roman Saxon shore fort at Portchester (or Portus Adurni). Much of it is still standing, reputedly having the most complete Roman walls to exist in northern Europe. The Norman castle is a quadrangular enclosure with a great tower, the enclosure's north and west sides are provided by the old Roman wall and the tower is built into the corner. A moat was cut outside the east and south enclosure walls. The tower, still existing, was built about 1100 during the reign of Henry I with 12th- and 14th-century additions. It was used to house prisoners of war during the Napoleonic Wars in the 18th and 19th centuries. An Augustinian priory was founded in the southeast corner of the Roman fort in the 1130s, and the church remains.

Strategic importance

A stragically important site, Portchester was well used: Henry I was a frequent visitor and both Edward III in the 14th century and Henry V in the next century assembled their armies here before setting out to do battle in France. Richard II transformed part of the castle into a small palace in the 14th century. Portchester's importance declined in the 15th century although in the Civil War the Parliamentarians billeted thousands of troops and detained prisoners of war here.

Visiting the castle

The keep houses an exhibition on the history of Portchester Castle and displays of the finds from archaeological digs on the site. The audio tour will enhance your visit to this site with its 2,000-year-old history. You can also access the Roman walls and the extensive grounds.

Location	Nr Fareham, Hampshire
Map ref	SU 625046
Tel	02392 378291
Web	www.english-heritage.org.uk
Open	Daily 10–6 Apr–Sep; 10–4 Oct–Mar

Powderham

More of a stately home than a castle now, Powderham (pictured below) has been home to the same family, the Courtenays, since the 16th century. Originally a fortified manor house built in the late 14th century, the castle was drastically remodelled in the 18th and 19th centuries after being damaged in the Civil War.

Visitor attractions

Today's visitors to the estate can enjoy a deer park and the grounds, where events are hosted throughout the open season, as well as the castle. Visit the chapel, state rooms and halls which are hung with tapestries and paintings. The Secret Garden with its animals will especially appeal to children as will the tractor and trailer rides.

Location	Kenton, Nr Exeter, Devon
Map ref	SX 968836
Tel	01626 890243
Web	www.powderham.co.uk
Open	Sun–Fri 10–5.30 Apr–Oct

Restormel

Restormel is a very fine example of a shell enclosure castle raised on an earlier motte. There are substantial remains of this enclosure, which was almost completely circular, 2.5m (8ft) thick and erected c.1200. A ring of apartments of stone and wood was raised around the inside of the shell. These included a kitchen, great hall, solar and barrack room for retainers. Edward, the Black Prince lived in the castle for a time. The already abandoned castle was garrisoned by the Parliamentarians during the Civil War but was never occupied again.

After exploring the ruins, if the weather is good, you can picnic while enjoying the picturesque surroundings. Please note that access to the castle is via an animal grazing area and you will need suitable footwear.

Location	Lostwithiel, Cornwall
Map ref	SX 104614
Tel	01208 872687
Web	www.english-heritage.org.uk
Open	Daily 10–6, Apr–Jun & Sep; 10–6 Jul–Sep ; 10–4 Oct

Richmond

This is an interesting early castle that dominates Swaledale from a great height, but never saw military action. The site was granted to Alan the Red in the 1080s and he erected a triangular curtain and possibly one of the earliest stone hall keeps in England, known as Scolland's Hall. This might have been built soon after Alan's death in 1089 but the name comes from Alan the Red's steward, Scolland.

History

The gate-tower was also begun in the 11th century, and appears to have been similar to the one at Exeter in Devon. Joining the hall on the extension of the curtain is the massive keep: the lower part is 11th century, the remainder from the 13th century. It was built as an extension of the original gate-tower *c.*1150–70, and it reached 30.5m (100ft), retaining the fine archway of the earlier gateway. The tower was built by Conan 'the little' Earl of Brittany.

Henry II took the castle after Conan's death and may have altered the tower more as he carried out various other alterations. By the early 16th century the castle was decaying, but it was converted into a military headquarters in 1855 and was in use during both world wars.

Visitors

The exhibition centre presents Castle, Commerce and Conscience – the history of the castle from fortress to prison. The Cock Pit garden has a grassed area for events and sitting out.

Location	North Yorkshire
Map ref	NZ 172007
Tel	01748 822493
Web	www.english-heritage.org.uk
Open	Daily 10–6 Apr–Sep; Thu–Mon 10–4 Oct–Mar

Rochester

Rochester stands on an important site where the Roman Watling Street crosses the River Medway. The first motte castle, mentioned in the Domesday Book, was held by the Conqueror's half-brother, Odo, Bishop of Bayeux, but taken in 1088 by William Rufus when Odo surrendered and returned to France.

The stone castle

Gundulf, Bishop of Rochester, began the first stone castle here. A stone curtain was built, probably c.1088, but the keep wasn't constructed until c.1127. At this time Henry I granted Rochester Castle to Archbishop William de Corbeil and his successors at Canterbury and gave him permission to build a tower. In 1215, King John took the castle after a long siege: he undermined the south corner turret and it collapsed.

The castle was rebuilt in a cylindrical shape with the addition of a drum tower. Further damage was inflicted when Simon de Montfort attacked in 1264. However, the garrison held out for the king. Edward III carried out repairs and restoration in the 14th century but the castle was later abandoned and fell into decay.

The remains are substantial and you can climb to the battlements and make out the plan inside.

Location	Kent
Map ref	TQ 741686
Tel	01634 402276
Web	www.english-heritage.org.uk
Open	Daily 10–6 Apr–Sep; 10–4 Oct–Mar

Rockingham

Rockingham is mentioned in the Domesday Book. It was a motte castle built by William the Conqueror on a steep hill overlooking the Welland valley, with two quadrilateral baileys. The early castle was probably residential rather than military but it was still an important site. The Great Council of Rockingham was held here in 1095. In the same year, Archbishop Anselm had one of his periodic confrontations with William II, which resulted in a trial before the king's court.

History

The castle was taken over by Henry II *c.*1156 and from then on, over at least two centuries, many new works and repairs were recorded. Among the major features of the castle is its twin cylindrical-towered gatehouse built by Edward I (c.1280–90) and still an impressive sight. Little of the original Norman castle remains and the main influence today is of the Tudor period. Henry VIII granted the castle to Edward Watson, an ancestor of the present owner and he converted the castle into a more comfortable mansion.

Charles Dickens was a frequent visitor here and used it as a model for Chesney Wold in his novel *Bleak House*.

Attractions

The castle displays a fine collection of 20th-century paintings among its many treasures, and hosts many events including jousting and open-air drama productions. The grounds are particularly splendid and guided tours are offered. There is a tea shop for refreshments. Visit the website for more information.

Location	Nr Corby, Northamptonshire
Map ref	SP 867913
Tel	01536 770240
Web	www.rockinghamcastle.com
Open	Sun & holiday Mon 12–5 (castle at 1pm) Easter–Apr; Sun, Tue & holiday Mon 12–5 May–Sep

Sandal

One of the most dramatic castle excavations of the 20th century revealed the ruins of a complete medieval castle here, which had all but disappeared in 2.5ha (6 acres) of earth and scrub.

Investigating the past

Sandal began as a motte castle c.1150, built by William de Warenne who received the Manor of Wakefield from Henry I, and substantial traces of timber buildings, including a hall, were found in the excavations. In c.1200 conversion to stone began and continued to about 1280. One of the early stone buildings is the barbican dated c.1250. The masonry round its base is of the highest quality, cut and beautifully shaped.

Property of the Crown

The de Warennes held the castle until 1361, when it became a possession of the Crown. Remains of a complex keep, added in 1484 by Richard III, were uncovered: Richard developed the castle as a suitable northern

base but despite its royal patronage, the history of Sandal was relatively uneventful, although the Battle of Wakefield was fought below the castle in 1460. The castle appears to have been neglected from the end of the 15th century, and entirely unoccupied from about 1600. It was refortified and garrisoned by Royalists in the Civil War, besieged twice in 1645, and then ordered to be slighted the following year.

Visiting

Finds from the castle site are on display at nearby Wakefield Museum but the on-site visitor centre has exhibitions on the castle. Refreshments are available.

Location	Nr Wakefield, West Yorkshire
Map ref	SE 337182
Tel	01924 302703
Web	www.wakefield.gov.uk
Open	Grounds dawn–dusk. Visitor centre daily 11–4.30 Apr–Sep; Sat–Sun 11–4 Oct–Mar

Scarborough

Standing proudly on a cliff edge are the ruins of the important northern royal power base of Scarborough Castle, begun in the 1130s by William le Gros, Count of Aumale. He built a stone curtain and the first stage of the great tower. The curtain together with the steep slopes of the cliffs formed a roughly triangular site.

Claimed by the Crown

Then in 1154 Henry II claimed Scarborough for the Crown, improved the fortifications and raised the keep on the site of the first tower. It is now ruinous, but was a square building, rising to over 30.5m (100ft) and built of rough stone and mortar, faced with fine ashlar laid in beautiful courses. King John made further improvements but the castle is noted for its barbican, built by Henry III in the 1240s.

War damage

Scarborough remained a royal castle until the reign of James I. A bombardment by Parliamentarians during 1645 badly damaged the keep, and after the Civil War the castle was used as a prison and barracks. The barracks were virtually destroyed during a shell attack in 1914. The castle was the site of a secret listening post during World War II. Walkways give access to wonderful coastal views.

Location	North Yorkshire
Map ref	TA 050892
Tel	01723 372451
Web	www.english-heritage.org.uk
Open	Open daily 10–6 Apr–Sep; Thu–Mon 10–4 Oct–Mar

LIFE IN A MEDIEVAL CASTLE

CASTLES WERE SYMBOLS OF STRENGTH AND CONQUEST, AND THAT SYMBOLISM REMAINED POWERFUL, BUT AS STABILITY INCREASED AND AS SOCIETY DEVELOPED, CASTLES BEGAN TO EXPRESS THE ASPIRATIONS OF THEIR OWNERS IN DIFFERENT WAYS.

By the 13th century many lords preferred to have their chamber and hall not high in a tower, but in a range of buildings within a central courtyard. These were nearly always timber-framed rather than of stone, and often these do not survive, making it difficult to imagine what they looked like. However, the Tower of London retains a few such buildings, as does Warwick, where great efforts have been made to re-create the feeling of life in the Middle Ages.

Notions of living in a civilized way spread, and so the castle courtyard often contained a garden where herbs and flowers would be grown. Here also, in good weather, minstrels might entertain and knights might court the ladies.

Many castles had moats around them. Originally, these were purely defensive in function, but they could also provide fish for food. But sanitation was problematic in castles, and so garderobes – lavatories – often consisted of a seat with a funnel channelling the waste down the walls and into the water. Where there was no moat, the waste was collected from the foot of the walls and taken to be used on the fields as manure. Clean water was usually taken from wells within the castle walls, but for daily use most people drank watered wine or 'small' beer – a weak beer that could be consumed without becoming drunk.

Furnishings and fittings became richer and more widespread. The lord and lady would have had a large bed with drapes and hangings closed around it.

Hangings were used to disguise bare stone walls and to keep out draughts. But one of the greatest luxuries came to be glass in the windows.

In the hall, centre of castle life, communal eating was still the norm, but kitchens gradually replaced cooking over fires in the hall itself. Rushes remained the best floor covering, since these could be easily replaced when soiled by food remains. A favourite floor covering was meadowsweet; it is gently scented and could disguise less pleasant smells. Weapons, armour and coats of arms would be displayed on the hall walls, twinkling in the fire glow.

St Michael's Mount

This granite outcrop, rising out of the sea in one of the southernmost bays of the Cornish coastline, has long held a position of strategic importance. St Michael's Mount was known as a safe harbour, a place of pilgrimage and an important trading port, long before any stone fortifications were built and was probably the island known as Ictis to the ancient Greeks, who traded for Cornish tin in the area. It certainly continued as an important port during the Roman occupation of Britain.

A Benedictine abbey

In the early 11th century, the Mount was occupied by a priest. However, after the Norman Conquest, Robert, Count of Mortain, became Earl of Cornwall, and granted the Mount to the Benedictine abbey at Mont St Michel. In 1135 the Abbot of Mont St Michel built a church on the Cornish outpost and established a religious community. It is likely that the tower survives from this first church, consecrated in 1144, but the rest of the structure was rebuilt in the 14th century. It is still used as a place of worship today.

In the early 15th century, Henry V declared war on France and in 1424 Henry VI granted the Mount to Syon Abbey.

The Armada

In 1588 the Spanish Armada was spotted in Mount's Bay and the first of a series of beacons was lit on the Mount to warn Sir Francis Drake in Plymouth. The Mount had experienced episodes of military activity from the late 12th century onwards, including a lengthy siege during the Wars of the Roses.

Civil War

In 1640, two years before the Civil War, Sir Francis Bassett, who became a leading Royalist commander in Cornwall, bought the Mount.

He spent large sums on gun batteries and other defences and was responsible for constructing the fortified gateway and watchtower on the main approach to the castle. The Mount is one of the best-preserved Civil War sites.

The St Aubyn family

The Mount finally fell to the Parliamentarians and in 1647 Colonel John St Aubyn became military governor. He purchased the Mount 12 years later. Successive generations of St Aubyns have restored the chapel, which had been used as an ammunition store during the Civil War, and gradually converted the rest of the castle for use as a private house.

Between 1873 and 1878, John St Aubyn, later the first Lord St Levan, built the spectacular East Wing, with his cousin Piers St Aubyn, as architect. In 1954, most of the island was given to the National Trust, although the St Aubyn family retained a 999-year lease to live in the castle and a licence to operate the visitor business in partnership with the Trust.

Visitor attractions

A weapons collection, Chippendale furniture, silverware and paintings are displayed. The garden features terraces of subtropical plants. Access to the Mount is by foot across the causeway or by motor boat at high tides in the summer. The climb to the castle is steep and paths may be slippery. There is a restaurant.

Location	Marazion, Cornwall
Map ref	SW 515298
Tel	01736 710507 (tide details 01736 710265)
Web	www.stmichaelsmount.co.uk
Open	Castle Sun–Mon 10.30–5.30 late Mar–Oct. Garden Mon–Fri 10–5.30 May–Jun; Thu–Fri 10–5.30 Jul–Oct

Scotney

The very small cylindrical turret at Scotney with machicolation and a conical roof is the main feature of a late 14th-century fortified manor house. Surrounded by a moat the castle was originally flanked by three other islands on which similar turrets stood. Designed by Roger Ashburnham, Conservator of the Peace in Kent and Sussex, the remaining turret retains his name, and is known as the Ashburnham Tower. The castle was later adjoined by a range of domestic buildings dating mostly from the 17th century. The ruins of these buildings along with the tower now form the focal point of the magnificent gardens laid out in the 1830s by Edward Hussey III.

Enjoy walks in the gardens with seasonal displays of azaleas and rhododendrons and roses as well as fine shrubs and trees.

Location	Nr Lamberhurst, Kent
Map ref	TQ 688353
Tel	01892 891081 (office) 01892 893820 (general information)
Web	www.nationaltrust.org.uk
Open	Old Castle Wed–Sun 1–5.30 May–Sep. Garden and shop Wed–Sun 11–6 mid-Mar to Oct

Sherborne Old Castle

The old castle at Sherborne stands in parkland, landscaped in the 18th century by 'Capability' Brown, across the lake from a grand Elizabethan mansion built by Sir Walter Raleigh in 1594. Raleigh, who stopped here en route to Plymouth, was so taken with the castle and its location that he petitioned Elizabeth I for the estate. He tried to convert the 12th-century fortress into a suitable dwelling but eventually built an entirely new home. The now ruinous old castle was designed on a grand scale by the powerful Roger de Caen, Bishop of Salisbury and Chancellor of England during Henry I's reign. He also built the abbey in the town.

The ruins of Old Sherborne Castle stand just 1km (0.5 mile) outside the town of Sherborne.

'Malicious and michievous'

A Royalist stronghold during the Civil War, it was dismantled after it fell to Parliamentary forces following a 16-day siege which led Cromwell to describe old Sherborne Castle as 'malicious and mischievous'.

Today's ruins are extensive and occupy a lovely site.

Location	Dorset
Map ref	ST 647167
Tel	01935 812730
Web	www.english-heritage.org.uk
Open	Tue–Thu and Sat-Sun 10–5 late Mar–Jun, Sep; Tue–Thu and Sat–Sun 10–6 Jul–Aug; Tue–Thu and Sat–Sun 10–4 Oct

Sizergh

Sizergh Castle started its life as a solar tower about 18.5 x 12m (60 x 39ft), built in the mid-14th century for defensive purposes. South of the tower is a rectangular turret called the Deincourt Tower, named after the original owners of the land, and both towers are battlemented. The Deincourt Tower had a dungeon at ground level.

The Strickland family

The castle has been in the possession of the same family, the Stricklands, for well over 700 years after a Deincourt married a Strickland in the 13th century. A great hall was added in 1450 and forms part of the entrance hall of the house today. Sizergh is part 14th-century tower, and part Tudor, part Elizabethan mansion. Further alterations were made in the 18th century when the great hall was enlarged.

Visiting the castle

The series of oak-panelled rooms are notable, in particular the Inlaid Chamber, a spectacular restoration with an ornate plaster ceiling. Sizergh has a fine collection of family portraits, furniture and large gardens, including lakes, which were laid out in the 18th century. Events include a tour through the garden with garden staff. The beautiful estate grounds are famous for their views of the Lake District. The remodelled shop and tea room are close to the car park.

Location	Nr Kendal, Cumbria
Map ref	SD 498878
Tel	015395 60951
Web	www.nationaltrust.org.uk
Open	Open Sun–Thu 12–5 Apr–Oct

Stafford

Stafford began as a large motte castle of c.1070. By the middle of the 12th century it was the property of the Stafford barony.

The great tower

Ralph, 1st Earl of Stafford, invited master-mason John of Burcestre to build a great tower on the old motte in 1347 and up went a rectangular core of three storeys with octagonal corner turrets rising an extra storey above. The upper storey contained a great hall and a great chamber. Rooms for the owners, wardrobes, chapel and garderobes were all in the tower.

'My rotten castle'

A century later, Stafford enjoyed its heyday as by then it belonged to Humphrey Stafford who had married into the Buckingham family. However, the 3rd Duke of Buckingham, Edward Stafford, was put to death by Henry VIII in 1521 and the castle was left to deteriorate. One owner early in the 17th century, referred to it as 'my rotten castle of Stafford'. It was slighted during the Civil War but the remains were reconstructed in the 19th century.

Visiting the ruins

Ruins of this rebuilding, together with medieval stonework and the earthworks of two large baileys, can still be seen. The site has been extensively excavated and details of the findings are displayed on interpretative panels on the site. There is a visitor centre and a full programme of events.

Location	Staffordshire
Map ref	SJ 902223
Tel	01785 257698
Web	www.staffordbc/gov.uk
Open	Open access. Visitor centre Tue–Sun & holiday Mon 10–5 Apr–Oct; Sun–Sat 10–4 Nov–Mar

Stokesay

Stokesay is one of the best-preserved medieval fortified manor houses in England. Built by the de Say family, the first structure was a simple two-storey 12th-century pentagonal tower with a projecting square wall-turret on the north angle, both with a timber-framed gallery.

Lawrence of Ludlow

In the late 13th century, the new owner, a rich wool merchant called Lawrence of Ludlow built a long hall with gabled windows on to the tower's south wall and at the south end of the hall a three-storey multi-angular tower; these buildings formed one side of an enclosure of stone which was surrounded by a moat. A charming Jacobean gatehouse was added in the 17th century.

Stokesay has survived in much the same condition as it was in its heyday.

A treat for visitors

Stokesay is a wonderfully evocative and romantic place to visit and is brought to life by the audio tour.

Location	Nr Craven Arms, Shropshire
Map ref	SO 436817
Tel	01588 672544
Web	www.english-heritage.org.uk
Open	Thu–Mon 10–5 Mar–May & Sep–Oct; daily 10–6 Jun–Aug; Fri–Sun 10–4 Nov–Feb

Tattershall

(accounts for the work survive and show that nearly one million bricks were made for Tattershall) but should also provide agreeable living accommodation. The large traceried window openings, a serious weak point during a siege, illustrate the shift in priorities from designing serious defensive strongholds to a style that was more illusionary and comfortable. However, the gatehouses, curtain walls and moat from the earlier castle would have provided defences if required. Tattershall passed to the Crown during the reign of Edward IV and then in the 16th and 17th centuries to the Earls of Lincoln, who eventually abandoned it as a residence.

Restoration

Lord Curzon, a vigorous campaigner for the preservation of Britain's ancient monuments, rescued the tower from complete ruination in 1910 and restored the tower. The property is now in the care of the National Trust and visitors can explore all the floors including the dungeons. The guardhouse contains a museum and there are exceptional views across the countryside from the battlements. Refreshments are available.

Tattershall Castle was first built of stone in the 13th century but just about all that remains now is the remarkable 15th-century great tower erected by Ralph, 3rd Baron Cromwell, Lord Treasurer to Henry VI from 1433 to 1443.

One million bricks

It is a masterly example of medieval brickwork, which was, at the time, a relatively new building material. Lord Cromwell intended that the tower should not only proclaim his status

Location	Lincolnshire
Map ref	TF 211575
Tel	01526 342543
Web	www.nationaltrust.org.uk
Open	Sat–Sun 12–4 early to mid-Mar & early Nov–early Dec; Sat–Wed 11–5.30 late Mar–Sep; Sat–Wed 11–4 Oct

THE ENGLISH CIVIL WAR

IF EVER THERE WAS A WAR THAT NO ONE WANTED, IT WAS THE CIVIL WAR OF 1642 TO 1646. THE CLOSEST THAT ENGLAND HAS EVER COME TO A REVOLUTION, IT WAS ABOUT DEEP AND PASSIONATELY HELD DIFFERENCES BETWEEN THOSE SUPPORTING THE MONARCHY AND THOSE WISHING TO EXTEND WHAT WE WOULD NOW CALL DEMOCRACY.

In a deeply conservative country, it was inconceivable to many to be disloyal to the king. For others, the king needed only to talk openly and to compromise.

The king's heartlands were in the West, Midlands and North; the parliamentary supporters had London as their core, with much of the South and East in support. But individual towns and cities might be in either 'camp', depending upon their local leaders.

Many areas tried to be impartial, and did their best to keep out both sides. As the conflict spread, their position became impossible, and eventually, almost every part of the country became embroiled. As all attempts at agreement collapsed, armed conflict seemed to be the only option and war began.

Prevented from entering London, the king and his army made Oxford their southern base. The king's armies and the Parliamentarians (popularly known as 'Roundheads') ranged far and wide over the country, fighting for territory. Ports were hotly contested, as they could provide supplies, arms and much else from other parts of the country and from abroad. There were critical nodal points and strategically important places that were fought over time and again. Castles became as important as they had been in medieval times. Some castles held out for very long sieges.

Oliver Cromwell emerged from the Parliamentarian army as a bold, clever and ruthless soldier, but it was not clear for a long time that he would eventually replace the king.

The war ranged back and forth, with battles lost and won on both sides. Eventually the king was captured. He was tried, sentenced to death, and beheaded on 30 January 1649.

Cromwell became 'Lord Protector', whose 11-year 'reign' achieved virtually nothing except to earn him almost unanimous vilification. When the monarchy was restored in 1660, with Charles II as king, there was widespread and genuine jubilation. But nothing could ever be quite the same again.

Tintagel

Best known for its associations with King Arthur and its spectacular setting, the castle sits on a headland silhouetted against the cliffs of the wild north Cornish coast. Much has fallen into the sea over the years, but the remaining visible ruins are of the castle built by Richard, Earl of Cornwall in the middle of the 13th century. It is divided in two by an isthmus between the headland and the mainland.

Arthur's castle?

Developed after the claim by medieval author Geoffrey of Monmouth that Tintagel was the birthplace of King Arthur, and with little economic or military importance, it seems the castle's existence was merely to associate the Earls of Cornwall with King Arthur. But, there was a fortification of some kind here in the 5th and 6th centuries, just at the right time for King Arthur, as excavations have revealed.

But who was here or why is unknown. The present castle was in ruins by the end of the 15th century.

For visitors

There is a climb of more than 100 steps up to the castle, and the surface is uneven and can be slippery, but you are rewarded by the atmosphere and views. If you have time, visit Merlin's Cave at the base of the castle cliff, and drop into the information centre in pretty Tintagel village.

Location	Cornwall
Map ref	SX 049891
Tel	01840 770328
Web	www.english-heritage.org.uk
Open	Daily 10–6 Apr–Sep; 10–5 Oct; 10–4 Nov–Mar

Totnes

Founded by Judhael de Totnes one of William the Conqueror's knights, the castle here began as a simple example of the most usual type of Norman fortification. However, Totnes is noteworthy for one of the largest mottes (mound) and best-preserved stone 'shell' enclosures in the country. Artificially constructed from pounded earth and rock and covered with a layer of clay, the motte, topped with its almost circular shell keep, dominates the pretty and ancient market town beneath.

Later in history

Earthworks are the only remains of the original 11th-century structure, which had a square wooden tower on top of stone foundations: the stone keep was added in the early part of the 13th century and was rebuilt, with crenellations, in the next. As in earlier times, when the local population had capitulated to the Norman invaders, Totnes offered no resistance to the Parliamentary forces in 1646, and the castle remains are substantial.

Totnes itself is one of the best towns to visit in the West Country, full of interesting old buildings and a fascinating variety of shops as well as a museum.

Location	Devon
Map ref	SX 800605
Tel	01803 864406
Web	www.english-heritage.org.uk
Open	Daily 10–5 Apr–Jun & Sep; 10–6 Jul–Aug; 10–4 Oct

Tower of London

The most famous of England's castles was begun soon after the Conquest, and built with one purpose: to overawe the inhabitants of the country's most powerful city. After the Battle of Hastings, the defeated English army had fled to London, and it was imperative for the Conqueror to act quickly to secure the city: he immediately ordered the construction of a castle on a site on the north bank of the River Thames, in the southeast corner of the Roman city walls. By the 1070s the first wooden buildings were being replaced with a huge stone tower. Once finished, its fearsome outline dominated the landscape of London and, as intended, its Anglo-Saxon population. Nothing like this had been seen in Britain before.

A model fortress

The noted castle builder and architect, Gundulf, Bishop of Rochester is thought to have designed the White Tower, as it became known after Henry III had it painted white. This massive, intimidating structure was a model for many other great towers and castles that have played a part in Britain's history.

By the middle of the 14th century the fortress had taken on the basic concentric plan that still exists today. It was vastly extended during Henry III's reign and again by Edward I, the two monarchs spending the equivalent of millions of pounds on improvements. When Edward died in 1307, the Tower of London was England's most powerful castle and a lavish royal palace.

Different roles

Roles for the site were expanding: since Henry III's time it was used as a prison, and Edward I set up the Royal Mint here (which remained until early in the 19th century). He also

ENTRY TO THE TRAITORS GATE

initiated the castle's function as a treasury (the Crown Jewels were moved from Westminster Abbey in 1303) and as a place for storing records. Perhaps the strangest inhabitants were the exotic animals kept in the Royal Menagerie. As early as 1255 an elephant, presented to Henry III by Louis of France, lived in a purpose-built elephant house at the Tower. At one point, a 'white' bear was kept and taken for regular swims in the Thames.

History

One of England's greatest castle builders, Edward III, instigated only minor changes although he began to build the Wharf, which was completed by his successor, Richard II: a king who had to take refuge in the Tower when rebels wreaked havoc during the Peasants' Revolt in 1381. The stage for many of the pivotal events of the 15th century, the castle's sinister side was illustrated by the execution of Henry VI in 1471 and the supposed murders of the young Edward V and his brother in 1483. Then, with the accession of the Tudor monarchs, came the palace's last days as a royal residence. Instead the focus shifted towards its role as prison and place of execution; the turbulence of the Reformation ensured that a large number of political and religious dissenters were interned at the Tower, a situation that continued into the 16th century.

England's most famous castle

For nearly a thousand years, the White Tower, William the Conqueror's mighty keep, has remained the focus of England's most famous castle. Within its walls, in 1399, Henry Bolingbroke forced the abdication of Richard II and became King Henry IV; Anne Boleyn was crowned in 1533; Henry VIII's daughter Mary was betrothed by proxy to Philip of Spain in 1554. Today the White Tower houses displays from the Royal Armouries' collection.

Unique attractions

A highlight of any visit here is seeing the Crown Jewels, but there is so much more: the Bloody Tower; Traitor's Gate; the Scaffold Site and Tower Green where prisoners were executed; the ravens and yeoman warder guards. The medieval palace has reconstructed interiors and exhibitions that show how it looked when Edward I stayed here. Events at the Tower take place regularly. There is also a restaurant.

Location	London
Map ref	TQ 336804
Tel	0870 756 6060
Web	www.hrp.org.uk
Open	Tue–Sat 9–6, Sun–Mon 10–6 Mar–Oct; Tue–Sat 9–5, Sun–Mon 10–5

Warkworth

A late motte castle of the mid-12th century, this eventually developed into a masterpiece of late medieval architecture and was the household of the most powerful family in the North. One part of the castle was ranged around the outer bailey and the other was contained within a magnificent multi-angular keep. Henry, son of David I of Scotland, probably built the earliest castle but it was the English Clavering (or FitzRoger) family who built the great gateway and massive curtain with flanking towers.

Early plumbing

By the end of the 13th century the castle was visited by Edward I. Warkworth was granted to the de Percys in 1332. The de Percys built the polygonal Grey Mare's Tail Tower and much later, in the 14th century the keep was erected: its apartments were grouped round a square lantern turret which ingeniously collected rainwater, channelled it to a tank in the basement and then distributed it to garderobes and basins. The keep is still a magnificent sight. The de Percys remained at the castle until the Reformation when the castle was pillaged. In the 19th century Anthony Salvin carried out some restoration.

For the visitor

This is a wonderful castle to explore, many of the walls have gone but the remains allow you to imagine Warkworth when it was a place of power and wealth. Refreshments are available on the site.

Location	Northumberland
Map ref	NU 247058
Tel	01665 711423
Web	www.english-heritage.org.uk
Open	Daily 10–6 Apr–Sep; 10–4 Oct; Sat–Mon 10–4 Nov–Mar

Winchester

The castle developed from 1067 until the beginning of the 14th century when, badly damaged by fire, it was more or less abandoned. Its ruins were finally demolished after the Civil War and only the splendid great hall, started by Henry III in 1222, survives.

A splendid capital

As capital of England from Saxon times until the end of the 12th century, Winchester was a favoured royal residence. King John spent a memorable Christmas there in 1206: 1,500 chickens, 5,000 eggs, 20 oxen, 100 sheep and 100 pigs were laid on for the festivities. The castle was captured by Louis of France in 1216, and Henry III (sometimes known as Henry of Winchester) was born at the castle and baptized in the cathedral; he spent about £10,000 on improvements and restoration. He built the surviving great hall on the site of an earlier structure; it still houses a huge Arthurian Round Table, built for Edward I and painted for Henry VIII.

Wolvesey

Nearby was one of the great medieval buildings of Europe, the ecclesiastical castle-palace at Wolvesey, built by Henry of Blois, Bishop of Winchester, c.1129–c.1171. It was a quadrangular castle with a square great tower and a great hall. Mary I and Philip of Spain held their wedding breakfast here after marrying in the cathedral. The 12th-century palace was ruinous after the Civil War but is worth visiting.

Location	Hampshire
Map ref	SU 477294
Tel	01962 846476
Web	www.hants.gov.uk
Open	Daily 10–5 Mar–Oct; 10–4 Nov–Feb. Closed occasionally for civic events

FOOD AND DRINK

In medieval castles, eating and drinking was at the heart of social life, most meals taking place in the great hall. Here, everyone gathered to eat and, on special occasions, to be entertained.

At feasts, a great variety of dishes and courses would be served, with the cooks trying their best to make the food taste good as well as making it look interesting. Swans might be served up re-clothed in their feathers and stuffed with dozens of smaller birds. Sweet dishes made of sugarpaste might be presented as elaborate sculptures depicting well-known stories and myths.

Meat was the central part of most meals, with venison being considered an especially luxurious food. Fish was eaten in large quantities, because meat was forbidden on Tuesdays, Fridays and Saturdays, as well as on special days. Moats were well stocked with fish and they were also bred in special pools.

Everyone – including children – drank alcohol. It was safer than water as the ingredients were boiled as part of the brewing process. Beer came in two sorts – 'single' ale or small beer, which was weak, and 'double' ale which was strong. All were consumed in large quantities – soldiers were given three litres (five pints) of wine a day.

Bread was a staple food. The rich would have eaten good-quality bread made with wheat flour, while the poor ate bread made with a mixture of barley flour, peas and beans. Castles usually had numerous bread ovens. Large numbers of people were entitled to eat at the monarch's expense, with bread being provided as part of their wages. For example, in King Stephen's reign, the Chancellor received each day one loaf of bread of the best quality, and two of ordinary quality, as well as one measure of good wine and one of ordinary wine, in addition to the meals he ate daily at the king's table.

Some special dishes were highly spiced. This was not because the taste needed disguising, but rather to show how wealthy the lord was, since he could afford to let his cooks use costly and rare herbs and spices.

Salt was an essential part of food preservation in medieval times, and was the main way to keep meat fresh. Meat was also preserved by smoking in chimneys.

Warwick

As medieval castles go, Warwick has to be one of England's most evocative, redolent of the history that shaped it since William the Conqueror first built his motte and bailey fortress here in 1068.

The Earl of Warwick

William's mound is all that survives of that fortification but over the centuries the castle grew into an impressive stronghold to reflect the status of its owners. By 1088 this was the seat of the Earls of Warwick who were to become significant figures in Britain's story.

By the middle of the 13th century the castle had an imposing gatehouse inserted into its stone curtain and a shell keep crowning the motte. The main protagonist in the the Barons' War, Simon de Montfort, lived at neighbouring Kenilworth Castle, so attack was almost inevitable when Warwick sided with Henry III.

Four years later the de Beauchamps inherited the earldom: it was Guy de Beauchamp who helped to seize and trick Edward II's favourite, Piers Gaveston, leading to Gaveston's trial and execution at Warwick in 1312. Early in the 15th century the family's influence at Court was great enough for Henry V to appoint Richard de Beauchamp as tutor to his son Prince Henry (Henry VI).

Kingmaker

The dynasty ended in 1449 when Richard Neville gained the title through marriage. So great was Neville's influence over the English monarchy that he was called 'Kingmaker'. After Neville was killed at the Battle of Barnet in 1471, the castle entered a period when it was affiliated even more closely with the

Crown. Through the 14th and 15th centuries Warwick was greatly extended with works that included the construction of Guy's Tower and a barbican. Under royal ownership the castle was embellished further.

In 1547 Warwick was granted to another influential family, the Dudleys, key players in the Lady Jane Grey/Mary Tudor struggle and powerful throughout the reign of Elizabeth I. The Dudleys' possession of Warwick ended in 1590. Early in the 17th century the castle passed into the hands of the Rich and Greville families who inhabited Warwick up to the end of the 20th century. It was lavishly refurbished in the 18th century, and the peerless landscaper 'Capability' Brown was commissioned to design the grounds.

A top visitor attraction

In 1978 Warwick was sold by the Grevilles to The Tussauds Group, which has put much effort into restoring and developing the castle, now one of Britain's top visitor attractions. Displays in the castle include period furnishings and the extraordinarily lifelike waxwork models, and show the life of the castle through the ages up to the late Victorian era. Parts of the medieval castle are incorporated into the state rooms, which were refurbished mainly in the 17th and 18th centuries. Today the castle is one of the best places in England to get a flavour of life in a medieval castle. There is a full calendar of events and the website is excellent. Restaurants serve refreshments.

Location	Warwickshire
Map ref	SP 284647
Tel	0870 442 2000
Web	www.warwick-castle.co.uk
Open	Daily 10–5 Jan–Mar, Oct–Dec; 10–6 Apr–Sep

Windsor

Windsor dates from *c*.1080 when William the Conqueror raised a motte fortress close to a royal hunting forest (now Windsor Great Park) as part of a string of defences around London. The layout of the fortress was a central motte with two flanking baileys; Arundel Castle has a similar plan, developed by the Normans for fortifications, which were built on a ridge. Both Henry I and Henry II began to expand the castle and stone was introduced to replace the wooden fortifications. The Round Tower, altered but still extant on top of William's motte, dates from 1170.

An iconic royal palace

It was during the reign of the great castle-building monarch, Edward III, in the 14th century that the castle at Windsor began its transformation into one of the world's most iconic royal palaces. Edward's massive Gothic architectural plan included the College of St George in the Lower Ward and a suite of royal apartments in the Upper Ward. He also established the chivalric Order of the Garter, which has always been associated with the castle at Windsor: St George's Chapel, in the Lower Ward, is the Order's spiritual centre. It was Edward IV who began building the

Chapel in 1475, and it was completed by Henry VIII in 1528. Many British monarchs are buried here including the family of Elizabeth II: her father George VI, the Queen Mother, and her sister, Princess Margaret.

Major developments

The next major period of development at Windsor was after the Civil War. Charles II and architect Hugh May spent 11 years altering the exterior of the castle and creating a series of splendid baroque state apartments. The Queen's Audience Chamber is perhaps the best preserved of Charles II's interiors although

many of the 17th-century baroque features were removed when George III inherited the throne and Windsor became his favourite residence. Work on the castle continued into the 19th century and George IV, with architect Jeffrey Wyatville, continued to transform Windsor in the Gothic Revival style. St George's Hall, used for state banquets, was created by George IV when he joined Edward III's Great Hall and Chapel to make one vast room. Windsor has remained much as it was after George IV carried out his remodelling. Queen Victoria, who used the castle as her principle residence, made few changes although it was during her reign that Windsor entered its heyday.

After a severe fire in 1992, 100 damaged rooms were restored to their original designs: rooms that were destroyed have been redesigned in a modern Gothic style, and thus the 20th century also contributed to this royal residence.

Visiting

You can go through the State Apartments (and at certain times the Semi State Rooms). There are collections of paintings, tapestries and porcelain and much more.

Queen Mary's Dolls' House with its attention to the minuteest of details is also on display at Windsor.

The superb website has details of family activities, closures, events and tours including details of opening days of the Semi State Rooms and St George's Chapel.

Location	Berkshire
Map ref	SU 970770
Tel	020 7766 7304
Web	www.royalcollection.org.uk
Open	Daily 9.45–5.15 Mar–Oct; 9.45–4.15 Nov–Feb

Scotland

Scotland's first castles were built by Normans, often at the invitation of the Scottish kings, and by the Scots themselves copying the idea. The 'classic' Scottish castle is the tower, a design that became widespread in the 14th century and was developed in the centuries that followed.

Strongly fortified residences were still being built in large numbers in Scotland after the majority of English castle owners felt able to relax and introduce such things as windows on outside walls. This was because Scotland could still be a dangerous and insecure place. Often the threats were from other Scots – intransigent Highland clans were frequent culprits.

Edinburgh and Stirling are Scotland's most famous castles. These two mighty complexes developed as royal palace-fortresses over many centuries and are unlike anything else in the country.

Aberdour

Aberdour is an assemblage of ruins from several periods. It began as a hall house built by Andrew Mortimer and passed through the Earl of Moray and the Douglas family until the 16th century when it belonged to the Regent Morton. After centuries of improvements the castle was damaged by fire towards the end of the 17th century and from then much of it was allowed to deteriorate.

Visiting
For today's visitors, there are substantial remains with a painted ceiling and a walled garden. Visitors will enjoy seeing the remains of the original tower house, one of the oldest still-standing masonry castles of Scotland. It is situated at the west end of the keep. A café is open in summer and on winter weekends.

Location	Fife
Map ref	NT 192854
Tel	01383 860519
Web	www.historic-scotland.gov.uk
Open	Daily 9.30–6.30 late Mar–Sep; Sat–Wed 9.30–4.30 Oct–late Mar. Last entries are 30 mins before closing time

Ardvreck

Perched on a rocky promontory jutting into the north side of Loch Assynt, Ardvreck (pictured opposite) is now a picturesque ruin. It was built in the 16th century as a simple rectangular tower with a cylindrical staircase turret at the southeast corner, corbelled out on the upper storeys. The three chambers on the ground floor were vaulted. After his defeat at Invercharron in 1650, the Marquis of Montrose, took refuge at Ardvreck, but was betrayed and handed over to Parliament, which hanged him in Edinburgh.

The castle was sacked in the 17th century. Although the ruin is too dangerous to explore, strolling through the captivating scenery of the surrounding countryside is most enjoyable.

Location	Nr Inchnadamph, Highland
Map ref	NC 239236
Tel	01383 860519
Web	www.historic-scotland.gov.uk
Open	Open access

Balvenie

Balvenie began as a substantial stone quadrilateral enclosure built by the Earls of Buchan in the 13th century. There are remnants of a small latrine turret on the north corner and of a larger square-plan tower on the west corner and of other buildings raised inside. The castle once belonged to the 'Black Douglases' but by the middle of the 16th century, it was owned by John Stewart, 4th Earl of Atholl, who completely remodelled the eastern part by constructing a palatial three-storey range with a cylindrical tower, which once had a 'pepper-pot' roof. The castle, occupied until the 18th century, changed hands many times; its last owner was William Duff.

For the visitor
Balvenie prides itself on offering an accurate insight into life in the keep several hundred years ago. Visitors will particularly enjoy the views from the top of the castle showing the entrance to the buildings and the moat surrounding them, and into the woods.

Location	Dufftown, Moray
Map ref	NJ 326408
Tel	01340 820121
Web	www.historic-scotland.gov.uk
Open	Daily 9.30–6.30 Apr–Sep

Blair

This is the palatial home of the Dukes of Atholl. It is largely a late 18th-century reconstruction grafted on to the remains of an earlier complex tower-house castle.

A private army

The first building was the Comyn Tower, built c.1270, later enclosed in a barmkin along with other buildings, including a lord's hall. 'Bonnie' Prince Charlie stayed here during the Second Jacobite Rising, and after the prince's flight, the castle was taken over by the Hanoverian government. Queen Victoria visited in 1844 and presented Colours to the Atholl Highlanders, Europe's last private army. The castle is still the home of the Dukes of Atholl.

Visiting

Today's visitors will find much of interest: walled gardens, arms and armour, paintings, furniture and memorabilia. Visitors with disabilities can follow a full tour of the castle through an audio-visual display.

Location	Blair Atholl, Perth & Kinross
Map ref	NN 866662
Tel	01796 481207
Web	www.blair-castle.co.uk
Open	Daily 9.30–4.30 Apr–Oct; Tue–Sat 9.30–12.30 Nov–Mar

Bothwell

Bothwell was an important castle and is still a fine ruin. It was built c.1270 by the Moray (later Murray) family who also owned Duffus Castle.

Partial building

The castle, built on the south bank of the Clyde in red sandstone, had a great tower, or donjon, over 20m (66ft) in diameter and at least 24.5m (80ft) high, with walls about 4.5m (15ft) thick. Although damaged, much of the donjon survives but the original castle was never finished. Foundations have been discovered of parts of a planned curtain wall, twin-towered gatehouse and other towers laid out to form a quadrilateral enclosure. Wide ditches also indicate that a large area was due to be fortified.

Chequered history

The castle changed hands often. In the 1290s it fell into English hands after the deposition of John Balliol in 1296 and the next year the Scots attacked and captured Bothwell after a 14-month siege. By employing a huge

'belfry' or siege tower made of prefabricated parts, Edward I successfully recaptured the castle in 1301. After Bruce's great victory at Bannockburn in 1314, the castle reverted to Scotland. Bothwell was captured by the English again c.1331, this time by Edward III who used it as a headquarters, but a few years later it fell into the Scottish hands of Sir Andrew Murray. Later in the 14th century the castle came into the possession of the 'Black Douglas' family who rebuilt the hall and chapel and erected a new wall from east to west.

Bothwell was finally abandoned in the 17th century but this large and substantial ruin is a joy to explore.

Location	South Lanarkshire
Map ref	NS 688593
Tel	01698 816894
Web	www.historic-scotland.gov.uk
Open	Daily 9.30–6.30 Apr–Sep; Sat–Wed 9.30–4.30 Oct–Mar

Brodick

The red sandstone Brodick Castle stands on the site of a Viking fortress. In the 13th or 14th century a stone L-plan tower house was built as a seat for the Dukes of Hamilton. The north wing is all that remains of the original building, and the remainder of the structure, dating mainly from the 19th century, was designed by Gillespie Graham.

Outstanding for visitors

A collection of furniture, paintings and sporting memorabilia is on display in the house, and the garden has an acclaimed rhododendron collection. The site is an outstanding example of how a stately home can embrace varied elements. The country park, which welcomes visitors all year round, is excellent.

Location	Isle of Arran
Map ref	NS 007379
Tel	01770 302202
Web	www.nts.org.uk
Open	Daily 11–4.30 (3.30 in Oct) Apr–Oct. Walled garden daily 9.30–5

SIEGES

CASTLES WERE PLACES OF REFUGE, AND THEY WERE BUILT TO WITHSTAND ATTACK, BUT NEARLY ALL CASTLE DEFENDERS WERE AFRAID OF SIEGES, WHICH COULD MEAN DEATH BY ATTACK OR STARVATION.

Capturing castles was an essential part of any war or campaign, as they controlled the surrounding lands.

Sieges could last for months, and this was the worst outcome for both defenders and attackers, as either side could become victim to bad weather, illness or starvation. So sieges were often avoided by negotiation, intended to reduce suffering on both sides.

If the siege was in earnest, the attackers might use siege engines to bombard the castle. The most powerful was the trebuchet, a giant catapult capable of firing stones as heavy as 136kg (300lb). Its range was not much more than 300m (328yds), but in skilled hands it could be formidably accurate, firing missiles right over the castle walls. The mangonel was less powerful. It could fire at, but not over, walls. Its advantage was its longer range.

These engines could also fire other things such as rotting animal corpses in the hope that they would spread disease, or the heads of captured defenders to demoralize the survivors.

Undermining walls was a threat to any castle not surrounded by water or built entirely on solid rock. Dover was attacked in this way in 1216, when the 'sappers' successfully brought down a gatehouse tower. But the defenders drove back the attackers and blocked the breach with rocks and tree trunks. The tunnel through the chalk can still be seen.

Other machines used during sieges were the cat, a battering ram housed inside a wheeled building for protection, and the belfry, a wheeled tower as high as the castle walls so that the attackers could jump directly into the castle.

Good, strong walls were usually the best defence the besieged could hope for, and walls could be as much as 10m (33ft) thick. Multiple defences helped, too, and castles became increasingly complex, culminating in the concentric castles with rings of outer 'curtain' walls overlooked by towers from which the defenders could fire arrows and throw stones. If one stretch of wall or even a tower was captured, the defenders could withdraw to other parts of the castle.

Caerlaverock

'Caerlaverock was so strong a castle that it feared no siege … it had but three sides round it, with a tower at each corner but one of them was a double one, so high, so long and so wide, that the gate was underneath it, well made and strong, with a drawbridge and a sufficiency of other defences'. This is a translation of *Le Siège de Karlaverock*, a contemporary French rhyming account of the siege in 1300 by Edward I.

The castle was built *c*.1280–1300 and held by the English for 12 years. The constable then declared for Robert Bruce, dismantling the castle as required by the Scottish king.

Caerlaverock was rebuilt in the 15th century, following the original design; the massive gatehouse was strengthened and made residential. Gun ports were inserted into the stonework for cannons and other small guns towards the end of the 16th entury. In 1630

Lord Nithsdale built a three-storey residential block against the inner eastern wall. The castle was defended for the king against the Covenanters in 1640. The ruins retain much of the formidable defensive building work

For the visitor

Visitors can see an exhibition on sieges or take a nature trail and there is an adventure playground for children. A café provides refreshments.

Location	Dumfries & Galloway
Map ref	NT 025656
Tel	01387 770244
Web	www.historic-scotland.gov.uk
Open	Daily 9.30–6.30 Apr–Sep; 9.30–4.30 Oct–Mar

Castle Campbell

This imposing complex of buildings round a well-preserved, rectangular tower is sited on a rocky mound in Dollar Glen. The tower was the earliest stone building and dates from the late 15th century, erected on what may have been a much earlier motte castle site.

With four storeys, three of which are vaulted, a pit prison and two entrances, the tower's floors were originally reached by straight-flight mural stairways. A square-plan stair tower with a spiral staircase was built in the 16th century. The ceiling was vaulted at a later date, probably the late 16th century and has masks painted in the stonework. The present roof, which is a much later

addition, has helped to keep the tower in such good condition.

The second building period was probably in the first half of the 16th century. The main work was a southern range outside the barmkin of the 15th-century tower. In the late 16th century a shorter range was added to the east, joining the original tower to the south range. A curtain at the west and northwest (with a gateway) completed the quadrangle.

These additions were ruined when the Royalists sacked Castle Campbell in the 1650s. The castle was a stronghold of the Campbells.

Visiting

Although the tower still stands, the adjoining rooms and halls are ruinous. The view across the countryside is excellent. The glen has a wonderful range of wildlife and is a Site of Special Scientific Interest.

Location	Dollar, Clackmannanshire
Map ref	NS 961963
Tel	01259 742408
Web	www.historic-scotland.gov.uk
Open	Open daily 9.30-6.30 Apr–Sep; Sat–Wed 9.30–4.30 Oct–Mar

The 15th-century, four-storeyed tower house is on the right in the view of Castle Campbell above.

Castle Donan

Also known as Eilean Donan, this much-photographed castle stands on an islet in Loch Alsh at the meeting point of three sea lochs and is joined to the mainland by an arched bridge. It is a major reconstruction of a strong, early 13th-century fortress built by Alexander II. Held by the MacKenzies and later the MacRaes, the original castle, a stone curtain enclosure that received a rectangular great tower, was a stronghold for the Jacobite cause. It was reduced to rubble by a bombardment from British frigates in 1719. Today's castle is the result of an early 20th-century reconstruction by Colonel Jon MacRae Gilstrap, a descendant of the original owners. It is recognizable as the setting of such films as *Highlander* and *The World is Not Enough*.

Attractions for the visitor

An exhibition sets the scene and reveals the early life of the castle. Visitors have access to most of the castle and guides can answer questions. You will see fine furniture, family portraits and Jacobite memorabilia. In the kitchens, models of staff from the 1930s prepare a banquet. Other rooms to visit include the Banqueting Hall, the Billering Room and the bedrooms. There is also a café.

Location	Dornie, Highland
Map ref	NG 881258
Tel	01599 555202
Web	www.eileandonancastle.com
Open	Daily 10-5.30 Apr–Oct

Castle Fraser

This is a rectangular tower castle first built in the 15th century. In the late 16th century it was converted to Z-plan and in the 17th century the main core was enlarged under the supervision of John Bell, a noted mason.

A 'luggie'

The diagonally opposing four-floor towers are cylindrical (southeast) and rectangular (northwest) and are equipped with ornamented shot-holes. There is also a 'luggie' between the vaulting of the hall and the chamber above, which was formed in the thickness of the wall and reached from behind a window shutter. An eavesdropper could slip into the cubicle by lifting a stone slab, replace it and listen to goings-on in the hall. The Cowdray family restored the castle early in the 20th century.

Plenty to see and do

The round tower offers stunning views across the estate. The rooms are richly furnished with 19th-century carpets and curtains, and portraits. You can see the Great Hall, the Victorian kitchen, secret stairs and more. The castle offers numerous activities to entertain visitors of all ages. The Woodland Secrets area is an ideal space for children to play safely among sculptures, bamboo figures and a stone circle. The 18th-century walled garden is under renovation and there is an organic vegetable garden, which sometimes supplies ingredients for soups cooked in the Victorian kitchen. A tea room provides refreshments.

Location	Kemnay, Aberdeenshire
Map ref	NJ 722125
Tel	01330 833463
Web	www.nts.org.uk
Open	Daily 11–5.30 Jul–Aug; Fri–Tue 12–5.30 Apr–Jun, Sep

Castle Stalker

Y ou can see this castle on a small island in Loch Laich from the road driving from Ballachulish down towards Oban. Access has always been by boat. The building was a rectangular tower house, about 14 x 11m (46 x 36ft), and with walls about 3m (10ft) thick. The entrance was at first-loor level, reached by a wooden ladder and later a stone stairway and the ground level contained a pit prison.

Stalker was probably built in the 15th century on the site of a 14th-century fortalice belonging to the MacDougalls. These MacDougall lands later became the property of the Stewarts until the 17th century when they passed to the Campbells after a wager.

Castle Stalker fell into disrepair and dereliction in the 19th century when the Campbells built a new home on the mainland, but it was preserved and then fully restored towards the end of the 20th century.

Visting

Visitors arrive by boat for tour of the castle accessed via steps from the beach.

The website has a very good virtual tour to whet your appetite.

Location	Appin, Argyll & Bute
Map ref	NM 921473
Tel	01383 860519
Web	www.castlestalker.com
Open	The Castle is open by appointment only. Please call the number given during the relevant period 6-10 Jun (01631 740 306) 13-17 Jun (01631 730 354) 22-26 Aug (01631 730 234) 29-2 Sep (01631 730 234) 5-9 Sep (01631 730 354) Tours are subject to tides and weather conditions

Cawdor

This palatial range of buildings belongs to the Dowager Countess Cawdor whose family has owned the castle since the 14th century. It was the seat of the Thanes of Calder.

Open to the king

The stone tower house was built c.1370 and crenellations and turrets were added to the tower in 1454, following a licence to fortify, granted to John Calder by James II of Scotland. This allowed him to erect his castle 'with walls and ditches and equip the summit with turrets and means of defence' on the understanding that it was always to be open to the king and his successors. The tower was substantial and the lower parts of it have survived, heightened in the 16th century. A ditch and a drawbridge were added in the 15th century. The first-floor entrance had a yett.

Visiting

Later improvements were residential and this comfortable castle displays a fine collection of furnishings, paintings, tapestries and domestic items. Its magnificent grounds have three gardens and a 9-hole golf course, which are all open to the public. There is also a restaurant.

Location	Highland
Map ref	NH 847499
Tel	01667 404401
Web	www.cawdorcastle.com
Open	Daily 10–5.30 May–Oct

Claypotts

Claypotts is one of several dozen Z-plan castles built in Scotland in the 16th and 17th centuries. John Strachan, Lord of Claypotts, built it in the 1570s as a rectangular, gabled, four-storey great tower house of local stone with cylindrical towers grafted diagonally on the northeast and southwest corners.

'Bonnie Dundee'

The towers were topped with overhanging square cap-houses and were large enough to contain rooms all the way up. Each of the towers gives cover to two surfaces of the centre building which in turn covers both towers so, in theory, it was impossible to approach the castle from any angle without being in a direct line of fire. However, the all-round defensiveness of Claypotts was never put to the test. In the 1620s the castle was sold to Sir William Graham of Claverhouse, and it was his great-grandson, John Graham, who was later famous throughout Scotland as 'Bonnie Dundee'. He became 1st Viscount Dundee, and raised an army to help the cause of James II (and VII) who was driven off the English throne late in 1688 by supporters of William of Orange. When James II was deposed, Claypotts was forfeited to William III who gave it to the Marquis of Douglas.

Visiting

Claypotts remains as an outstanding example of 16th-century Scottish architecture but visitors will usually only be able to enjoy the view from the grounds. Contact Historic Scotland for details of open days for viewing the interior, or visit their website.

Location	Broughty Ferry, Dundee
Map ref	NO 457319
Tel	01786 431324
Web	www.historicscotland.gov.uk
Open	Check with Historic Scotland

Craigievar

Craigievar, set high on a hill, is a fairy-tale castle and one of the finest baronial tower houses in Scotland. Built c.1610–26, internally Craigievar is simple and homey with a decorated and vaulted roof in the great hall. In fact, most of the rooms in the castle have retained their original 1626 ceilings.

A 17th-century castle

Built by William Forbes or 'Danzig Willie', it remains true to its 17th-century origins. The simplicity of the lower part of the castle contrasts with the finely corbelled, well-proportioned cylindrical turrets with conical roofs and cupolas above. Built as a defensible home rather than for purely military purposes, the castle was fortified with ramparts, and a courtyard wall with towers and an outer gateway. There was only one way into the castle – through a massive iron-studded door, past a yett and through another pair of stout doors.

Inside, the castle has been maintained as it was when the Forbes family left. Belongings collected by the family over the centuries include fine 17th- and 18th-century furniture and Forbes family portraits, as well as a renowned collection of early 20th-century ceramics.

For the visitor

Craigievar is undergoing restoration so the castle is closed; it is is planned to reopen in 2008. After this date, before planning a visit, please either telephone or check the website to ensure the castle has reopened.

Location	Alford, Aberdeenshire
Map ref	NJ 566095
Tel	013398 83635
Web	www.nts.org.uk
Open	Please check NTS website

Craigmillar

This castle (pictured right) is famous as the place where the murder of Darnley, husband of Mary, Queen of Scots, was planned while the queen was staying there in 1566–7. The castle began in the late 14th century as a large L-plan tower house and was built with close-texture rubble of red-grey sandstone, with long, dressed quoins. The great tower house was fortified in the 1420s by the addition of a massive fortified enclosure with round flanking towers, and other additions were made in the 16th and 17th centuries.

The murder plot

Craigmillar was attacked and burned by the Earl of Hertford on behalf of Henry VIII in 1544, but it was restored in time for Mary, Queen of Scots to reside there from 1566–7 after the murder of her secretary, David Rizzio. During her stay, a band of conspirators, Argyll, Huntly, Bothwell, Maitland and Gilbert Balfour, met and plotted to ensure that 'sic ane young fool and proud tirrane suld not reign nor bear reull over thame: and that … he sould be put off, by ane way or uther …': Darnley was to be dispatched.

For the visitor

The castle is an impressive and substantial ruin that invites exploration. You can still climb to the roof of the tower house and enjoy panoramic views.

Location	Edinburgh
Map ref	NT 283705
Tel	0131 661 4445
Web	www.historic-scotland.gov.uk
Open	Daily 9.30-6.30 Apr–Sep; Sat–Wed 9.30-4.30 Oct–Mar

Crathes

Crathes is an impressive and much restored tower-house castle known for some interesting painted ceilings, most notably in the Chamber of the Nine Muses.

Begun as an L-plan tower house in 1553, many of the alterations and improvements were by masons from the Bell family. There were further alterations, including a three-storey east wing, another later wing, and some ornamental corbelled turrets. The original tower was equipped with a 'luggie', an iron yett by the door and a re-entrant tower for a staircase.

Visiting

There are collections of family portraits and furniture displayed inside the house and a fine garden to enjoy with several nature trails, one of which is especially suitable for visitors with disabilities. Children will want to head for the adventure playground. A restaurant provides refreshments.

Location	Aberdeenshire
Map ref	NO 735968
Tel	01330 844525
Web	www.nts.org.uk
Open	Daily 10–5.30 Easter–Sep; daily 10–4.30 Oct; Thu–Sun 10–3.45 for guided tours Nov–Mar

Crichton

Crichton Castle is a formidable structure dating from several periods. Its buildings range round a square courtyard, and from the top of the old tower house it is possible to see Borthwick Castle, another fine tower house.

Various building periods

The castle now has little more than its walls but it is possible to trace the various building periods. The first structure was a rectangular tower house, probably built by John de Crichton towards the end of the 14th century and originally surrounded by a barmkin. The basement is vaulted, and has a prison cell and a kitchen. In the 15th century the once massive gatehouse tower at the southwest was built by John de Crichton's son, William, who became Lord Chancellor and who virtually managed Scotland during some of the minority of James II. Further alterations, including the addition of more buildings, were made in the 15th century.

The castle was besieged and captured in 1559 in the struggle between Protestants and Catholics during the Scottish Reformation. Later in the 16th century, Francis, Earl of Bothwell, a cousin of Mary, Queen of Scots, who had spent time in Spain and Italy, transformed the castle into a Renaissance mansion including a notable diamond-faceted stonework façade on the north range.

Location	Midlothian
Map ref	NT 380611
Tel	01875 320017
Web	www.historic-scotland.gov.uk
Open	Daily 9.30–6.30 Apr–Sep

Dean

Dean Castle, the historic seat of the Lords of Kilmarnock, is concealed within a valley where the Fenwick and Borland waters enter lowland Ayrshire. The Boyd family received the barony of Kilmarnock from Robert the Bruce, after their support during the Wars of Independence and the castle was gifted to the Burgh of Kilmarnock in 1975 by the 9th Lord Howard de Walden.

Restoring the castle

The building is now a museum and visitor attraction within Dean Castle Country Park. Described as the best example of a faithfully restored medieval castle in Scotland, Dean is a courtyard castle with a massive 14th-century fortified keep with separate and more palatial buildings next to it from the 15th century, all protected by an encircling curtain wall. In 1899 Thomas Scott-Ellis became the 8th Lord Howard de Walden and inherited the Kilmarnock Estate. A man of many interests and talents, he was in particular fascinated by the medieval past. Between 1908 and 1946 he restored the castle, which had lain a ruin since the 18th century.

Visiting

The castle now houses the 8th Lord Howard de Walden's own collections of arms and armour, and tapestries. Dean Castle is also home to an internationally important collection of early musical instruments assembled by the 8th Lord's father-in-law, Charles van Raalte. For refreshments there is a tea room in the country park visitor centre.

Location	Nr Kilmarnock, East Ayrshire
Map ref	NS 437394
Tel	01563 554708
Web	www.deancastle.com
Open	Wed–Sun 11–5 or by special arrangement

Dirleton

Dirleton began as an earth-and-timber castle built by the Norman de Vaux family who were encouraged to settle in Scotland by David I in the 12th century. Some time in the early 13th century a cluster of stone towers was built. The main structure was the cylindrical great tower, about 11.5m (38ft) in diameter and rising to three storeys.

In 1298 the castle was besieged on Edward I's orders. The garrison was compelled to surrender; but later it was retaken and then slighted by Robert Bruce.

In the 14th and 15th centuries the castle was converted into a more elaborate enclosure with ranges of buildings along the east, a more powerful gatehouse on the southeast (remains can be seen of this), and a block on the northeast.

During the 17th century Royalists used the castle as a refuge and in 1650, General Lambert besieged the castle on behalf of Cromwell and they slighted the buildings.

For the visitor

Although a ruin, the castle is still impressive and well worth visiting as there is plenty to see as you explore.

The castle gardens are a real attraction and have always been cultivated. The early 20th-century Arts and Crafts garden has what is claimed to be the world's longest herbaceous border.

You approach the castle ruins through the garden, where you will see the large beehive shaped dovecot, which would have supplied the castle with meat.

Location	East Lothian
Map ref	NT 516839
Tel	01620 850330
Web	www.historic-scotland.gov.uk
Open	Daily 9.30–6.30 Apr–Sep; 9.30–4.30 Oct–Mar

Doune

The name Doune is derived from 'dun', the ancient word for a fortified town and there are traces of prehistoric earthworks around this splendid stone enclosure castle. It was built towards the end of the 14th century for Robert Stewart, Duke of Albany and Regent of Scotland from c.1396 to 1420. When Albany died in 1420 his son, Murdoch, inherited the castle but he was put to death by James I in 1425 and Doune was taken over by the Crown. It was held for more than a century by royalty and then passed to the Earls of Moray who owned it until it was passed into the care of Historic Scotland in the 1980s.

Visiting the castle
The castle was restored in the first half of the

19th century and then again towards the end of the 20th century. The Duke's Hall, on the first floor above the gateway passage, is laid out much as it would have been in its heyday, and to the west is the vast great hall. The castle was one of the locations for the film *Monty Python and the Holy Grail*.

Location	Stirling
Map ref	NN 725014
Tel	01786 841742
Web	www.historic-scotland.gov.uk
Open	Daily 9.30–6.30 Apr–Sep; Sat–Wed 9.30–4.30 Oct–Mar

Drum

The castle at Drum is a fine example of a late 13th-century great tower, one of the three oldest in Scotland and the only one to remain intact. It has rounded corners and few window openings, a spiral staircase from the first floor up to the battlemented parapet and wall-walk, and adjoins an early 17th-century mansion built by the 9th Laird of Drum. The castle was further altered during Victorian times.

William Irvine, armour-bearer to Robert Bruce, was given the charter to the Royal Forest of Drum in the 1320s but it is likely that the tower was built before the 1280s. Its site, on a

ridge above the River Dee, would have afforded protection for nearby Aberdeen.

Visitor attractions
Irvine descendants passed the castle to the National Trust for Scotland in 1976. Inside there are fine portraits and a collection of Georgian furniture. The grounds contain a garden of historic roses, a pond garden and the Old Wood of Drum, an ancient oak wood that is now a Site of Special Scientific Interest.

The castle has a lively atmosphere largely due to the range of events held there, mainly geared to families. There is also a tea room serving refreshments.

Location	Nr Peterculter, Aberdeen
Map ref	NJ 796005
Tel	01330 811204
Web	www.drum-castle.org.uk
Open	Daily 12.30–5.30 Apr–May & Sep; 10–5.30 Jun–Aug Last entry 45 mins before closing

Drummond

The present keep at Drummond, seat of the Earls of Ancaster, was erected in 1490 by special permission of James IV. Built by Sir John Drummond, it was heavily damaged by Cromwell in the 1650s but rebuilt. The mansion house, today mostly Victorian, was built in 1689.

Drummond Castle is not open to the public but visitors can enjoy one of the finest formal gardens in Europe. Together with the multi-faced sundial, the property's most admired feature is its Italianate parterre garden from which visitors have wonderful views.

Location	Nr Crieff, Perth & Kinross
Map ref	NN 844180
Tel	01764 681433
Web	www.drummondcastlegardens.co.uk
Open	Gardens only. Easter Weekend and daily 1–6 May–Oct

Duffus

Founded by Freskin de Moravia, a Norman-Scottish baron in the reign of David I, Duffus began as a tall motte surrounded by a ditch with a ditch-encircled bailey. It was surrounded by marsh ground, which has now given way to flat farmland. Scottish patriots burned the wooden castle and c.1300, the motte was given a stone great tower and a stone curtain round the bailey. In the 15th century a range of buildings was added along the north side of the bailey.

The castle is now ruinous but it remains one of the finest examples of a motte and bailey castle in Scotland.

Location	Elgin, Moray
Map ref	NJ 189672
Tel	01667 460232
Web	www.historic-scotland.gov.uk
Open	Open access

ENTERTAINMENT AND SPORT

LIFE IN MEDIEVAL CASTLES WAS NOT UNREMITTINGLY GRIM. THERE WAS SINGING AND LAUGHTER, AND THERE WERE GAMES. JOUSTING AND HUNTING WERE FOR THE NOBILITY, BUT ORDINARY PEOPLE COULD WATCH THE JOUSTS, AND SOMETIMES ATTEND A FEAST.

The lord may have had a resident jester, and part of his job was to entertain during the long evenings, primarily by making people laugh. Travelling troubadours provided songs and music, often accompanied by harps, trumpets or fiddles. Storytelling was hugely important, and epic stories would be told around the fire. Especially loved were tales about chivalry and the brave deeds of knights. Stories about King Arthur were favourites.

Outside, an early form of soccer called camp-ball was played. Using a pig's bladder stuffed with dried peas, the idea was to score goals – as today – but there were virtually no rules and any number of players could join in. It was chaotic and dangerous.

Hunting was very popular with nobles; many different kinds of animal were hunted, but deer were the most prized. Large areas of countryside were set aside for hunting, the most well-known being the New Forest in Hampshire. Some smaller castles, such as Odiham, were used primarily as places from which to undertake hunts. Hares were considered to be good sport, partly because they were difficult to catch, and wild boars were also hunted, although these were very dangerous, especially when cornered.

Dogs were an essential part of the hunt, and nobles made a great fuss of their dogs, sometimes treating them better than their servants. Favoured hunting dogs slept by the fire in the hall.

Tournaments were among the most popular events. Here, knights would joust for rich prizes, watched by large numbers of onlookers. Jousting could be fatal, even though the lances were made to splinter on impact. To minimize the danger, knights wore heavy armour and helmets with narrow eye slits, but even this could be dangerous, so at the last moment the knight would raise his head. This made the slits safe from splinters, but meant that for the last few seconds the knight could not see where he was going. He had to rely on the momentum and steadiness of his horse. Some knights earned their living by travelling from tournament to tournament.

Dumbarton

Recorded as a stronghold for longer than any other site in Britain, the castle is built on Dumbarton Rock, a volcanic neck of basalt jutting out into the Clyde. There was a settlement here in 450 when St Patrick wrote a letter to the King of Strathclyde at Alcuith (Clyde Rock). By the early 13th century there is a reference to a 'new castle' on the site but the only surviving structure from then is the Portcullis Arch. The medieval history of Dumbarton is one of changing ownership, and it was besieged several times. During the 17th and 18th centuries most of the medieval buildings (which were ruinous) were replaced with the extant buildings. These provided a base for government troops during the Jacobite risings and to defend the Clyde against France.

Visiting

An exhibition of military regalia and unusual tombstones is on display. The battlements offer tremendous views but, be warned, there are a lot of steps if you visit the castle.

Location	West Dunbartonshire
Map ref	NS 398744
Tel	01389 732167
Web	www.historic-scotland.gov.uk
Open	Daily 9.30–6.30 Apr–Sep; Sat–Wed 9.30–4.30 Oct–Mar

Dunnottar

Dunnottar Castle sits on a flat-topped promontory surrounded by the North Sea and joined to the mainland by a small low-level isthmus. The approach is likely to be difficult for visitors with disabilities. The site of fortifications for hundreds of years, an earthwork and clay castle from the 12th century was used by William the Lion as an administrative centre. At the end of the 14th century an early L-plan tower house was built on the headland.

A grand residence

The castle was granted to the Earl Marischals of Scotland in 1531 by James V and became one of Scotland's most palatial residences in the late 16th and early 17th centuries. Besieged by Montrose in 1645 and again in 1651 by Cromwell's forces, Dunnottar was dismantled in the 18th century but the ruins are impressive and some repairs have been carried out.

During Cromwell's time at Edinburgh Castle, the Honours of Scotland, the crown, sceptre and sword of state, were hidden at Dunnottar Castle. This dramatic site, almost surrounded by the sea, was the location for *Hamlet* (1990) starring Mel Gibson.

Location	Nr Stonehaven, Aberdeenshire
Map ref	NO 881838
Tel	001569 762173
Web	www.dunechtestates.co.uk
Open	Mon–Sat 9–6, Sun 2–5 Easter–Oct; Fri–Mon 9–sunset Nov–Easter

Dunrobin

This magnificent castle-palace is largely the creation of the 17th and 19th centuries, built on an early 15th-century great tower, which belonged to the Earls of Sutherland (then Morays). The most northerly of Scotland's great houses, in the 17th century the tower was converted to a courtyard-plan castle-mansion. Sir Charles Barry remodelled it in the 19th century.

Splendid attractions

There is much for visitors to see here including paintings, furniture and heirlooms. Queen Victoria stayed here and her room, the Gold and Green Room, can be viewed. The study has secret stairways. Outside, the gardens were inspired by the grounds of Versailles, and Dunrobin itself recalls a French château. The museum in the grounds has a range of interesting exhibits. There is also a tea room offering a range of refreshments.

Location	Golspie, Highland
Map ref	NC 852008
Tel	01408 633177
Web	www.great-houses-scotland.co.uk
Open	Mon–Sat 10.30–4.30, Sun 12–4.30 Apr–May & Oct; Mon–Sat 10.30–5.30, Sun 12–5.30; Mon–Sun 10.30–5.30 Jul–Aug

Dunstaffnage

Dunstaffnage sits on a rock on the edge of the Firth of Lorne and on one side the rock face actully makes up part of the castle wall itself. The castle originally dates from the 13th century and was occupied until the end of the 1800s. Alexander II and Alexander III used the site during their campaigns against the Vikings in the Western Isles. Its importance as a checkpoint to the approach to Glen Mor was also recognized by Edward I. It was captured by Robert Bruce in 1309 from the MacDougalls, who sided with Edward I, and passed to the Campbell family via the first Earl of Argyll and then to his cousin, who became Captain of Dunstaffnage. The family retains ownership. Flora Macdonald was held here after she helped 'Bonnie' Prince Charlie.

Traditionally, Dunstaffnage is on the site of an earlier building of the ancient Kings of Dalraida, where the Stone of Destiny was kept until it was removed to Scone (from where it was removed by Edward I).

Visiting

The ruins of the castle and its 13th-century chapel, situated southwest from the keep, can be visited today. The wall walk has views across the area. Visitors can also enjoy the woodlands and areas leading to Dunstaffnage Bay.

Location	Oban, Argyll & Bute
Map ref	NM 882344
Tel	01631 562465
Web	www.historic-scotland.gov.uk
Open	Mon–Sun, 9.30–6 Apr–Sept; Sat–Wed 9.30–4.30 Oct–Mar

Dunvegan

This romantic fortress is still occupied by the Chiefs of the MacLeod clan whose ancestors erected it in the Middle Ages. The present structure is a 19th-century transformation of a castle begun in the 13th century and it is possible to see relics from many of the ten building periods. Dunvegan stands on a rock projecting into the sea. One early feature of the castle is the remnant of a sea gate, which was once the only entrance to the castle.

Attractions for the visitor

Displayed inside are MacLeod heirlooms including the bullhorn, which dates from the 14th century. It is still filled with claret for each male heir to the MacLeod Chiefdom who then has to drain it. The castle gardens were laid out in the 18th century. Today the gardens remain open throughout the year, attracting keen gardeners from around the world. A popular excursion is a boat trip to see the seals in Loch Dunvegan. The restaurant has ramps for wheelchair access.

Location	Isle of Skye
Map ref	NG 250480
Tel	01470 521206
Web	www.dunvegancastle.com
Open	Daily 10–5 mid-Mar–Oct; 11-4 Nov–mid-Mar

Edzell

Edzell began as a substantial rectangular L-plan tower house built by the Lindsay family in the early 16th century. Later a quadrangle of buildings was added and connected to the tower by an entrance hall, and in the first years of the 1600s, Sir David Lindsay added a spacious pleasaunce or walled garden to the eastern side of the courtyard. Sir David died before his project was completed, but the garden still exists. A bath-house tower and a summer house, which is still intact, were added to the corners of the highly decorated walls of the pleasaunce and the garden here is one of the most notable of any British castle.

A peaceful history

As a fortress, Edzell had a peaceful history and it was the scene of various royal visits, including one by Mary, Queen of Scots when she held a Privy Council meeting in the hall. Although fortified, the castle was never besieged but suffered through the misfortune of the families that owned it. Edzell was finally sold to the York Building Company and when it went into liquidation, the company assets, including Edzell, were stripped. The castle then passed into the hands of the Dalhousie family.

Visiting

Today it is an interesting and attractive ruin with a wonderful, well-maintained walled garden, which includes sculptures and carved panels.

Location	Angus
Map ref	NO 585691
Tel	01356 648631
Web	www.historic-scotland.gov.uk
Open	Mon-Sun, 9.30-6.30 Apr–Sep; Sat-Wed 9.30-4.30 Oct–Mar

Edinburgh

The history of Edinburgh's craggy fortress, entwined with that of Scotland itself, reaches back for thousands of years.

A major royal fortress

At the end of the 11th century this royal stronghold was known as the Castle of Maidens. During the reign of David I the castle emerged as a major royal fortress; it was here that the first recorded assembly of the forerunner of today's Scottish Parliament took place in 1140 and it was David I who built the tiny St Margaret's Chapel (named for his mother), which still exists as the oldest surviving building in the castle precincts.

Most of the buildings were rebuilt in stone during the 13th century before Edward I's campaign in Scotland. Nevertheless Edward captured the castle in 1296 and the great Scottish fortress fell, not for the first time or the last, into English hands. It was Robert Bruce's son, David II who then rebuilt the fortress after it was finally back in Scottish hands and remnants of the 14th century David's Tower still lie beneath the 16th-century Half-Moon Battery.

Symbol of the capital

Much of the medieval castle was destroyed in the 'Lang Siege' of 1571–3 and more still in the 17th century when Cromwell set up his Scottish headquarters here and the castle's role shifted from palace to garrison. Many of the castle's extant buildings date from this time and later, although the main courtyard, Crown Square, was begun during the 15th and 16th centuries. Built over vast stone cellars (used at various times to incarcerate prisoners of war) the square contains the most important castle buildings including the royal palace and great

hall. The creation of Edinburgh as the Scottish capital during the reign of James III meant that, like England's Tower of London, the fortress was to serve as the realm's chief arsenal, home to the Honours of Scotland and repository of the state archives.

Visiting the castle

The ancient Honours of Scotland – the Crown, the Sceptre and the Sword of State – are displayed in the Crown Room. Other highlights are the Stone of Destiny, Mons Meg, a medieval cannon presented to James II, the National War Museum and The One O'Clock Gun, fired daily from Mills Mount Battery. A newer exhibition, Prisoners of War, in the cellars re-creates the conditions for the sailors held here in the 18th and 19th centuries. Cafes provide refreshments. The views of Edinburgh from the battlements are magnificent.

Location	Edinburgh
Map ref	NT 252374
Tel	0131 225 9846
Web	www.historic-scotland.gov.uk
Open	Daily 9.30–6 Mar–Oct; 9.30–5 Nov–Feb

Elcho

Elcho is a much restored, massive five-floor tower house of the 16th century and is particularly fascinating for its tower attachments. A substantial square-plan tower projects from the southwest corner of the block with three more tower projections along the north wall, one square, one semi-cylindrical and one cylindrical. On the north wall of the block are three more tower projections, east to west.

Elcho's windows are protected by iron grilles and the walls have gun ports, but the castle was also designed to provide handsome family accommodation. There is evidence that the tower house was enclosed inside a barmkin with a ditch outside.

The nearby quarry, now a garden, was flooded and connected to the River Tay, and

this would have provided a private dock for the castle.

Visiting Elcho

Visitors can view the interior – the ground and second floors are intact – and go up to the rooftop walkway to enjoy views to the river Tay estuary and back up towards Perth from the upper tower.

Location	Nr Perth, Perth & Kinross
Map ref	NO 164210
Tel	01738 639998
Web	www.historic-scotland.gov.uk
Open	Daily 9.30-6.30 Apr–Sep

Fyvie

One of Scotland's great royal fortress-palaces, visited by both Edward I and Robert the Bruce, Fyvie has a long and complex building history. The whole south front has a formidable appearance, but is not actually properly fortified and the first mention of stonework at the castle is about 1390. The southeast tower (Preston) was built between 1390 and 1430; the southwest (Meldrum) tower, some time between 1433 and 1590. The gatehouse is from the late 16th century. Additions were made right up to the 1890s. This is a perfect example of a castle that continued to be lived in long after there was any need for it to have a defensive function.

Attractions for the visitor

Inside, the most famous and notable feature is the wheel staircase, with wide sweeping steps and a solid newel. It is the finest example in Scotland. The opulent interior has excellent collections of portraits and arms and armour. Fyvie's grounds were landscaped in the 19th century: the traditional walled garden has been preserved and is now stocked with fruits and vegetables. A tea room provides refreshments.

Location	Turriff, Aberdeenshire
Map ref	NJ 764323
Tel	01651 891266
Web	www.nts.org.uk
Open	Sat–Wed 12–5 Easter–Jun & Sep; daily 11-5 Jul–Aug

Glamis

This magnificent mansion of the Earls of Strathmore and Kinghorne, one of the finest in Scotland, conceals a number of earlier structures.

In 1372 Robert II granted the site to Sir John Lyon and in about 1400 the second Sir John began to build an L-plan tower house. This had outer defences of walls and flanking towers and was surrounded by a moat. Remains of the medieval castle are incorporated into the present castle, which evolved during the 17th and 18th centuries.

The Queen Mother

Glamis was the childhood home of the late Queen Mother, Lady Elizabeth Bowes Lyon. She married the future George VI in 1923 and was mother to Elizabeth II, and to Princess Margaret, who was born here.

Glamis features in Shakespeare's *Macbeth*, and Shakespeare himself may have visited the castle. It is reputedly haunted by a number of ghosts, and the young Lady Elizabeth and her brother David liked to dress in sheets to frighten visitors.

Today's visitors approach the castle along a spectacular mile-long avenue. The beautiful gardens were landscaped in the early 19th century and in addition to formal gardens, feature a nature trail and a pinetum, where you might spot a rare red squirrel.

The castle is still a family home, and visitors can join a tour of selected rooms. For anyone who is a fan of the 'Queen Mum' or of the royal family in general, a visit to Glamis is essential. There is a restaurant on the site.

Location	Angus
Map ref	NO 386480
Tel	01307 840393
Web	www.glamis-castle.co.uk
Open	Daily 10–6 Mar–Oct; 12–4 Nov–Dec

Glenbuchat

This late 16th-century castle was built on the Z-plan, with square towers, and belonged to the powerful Gordon family. One of its owners was John Gordon, a hero of both Jacobite Risings. Known as Old Glenbuchat, John Gordon's devotion to the Pretender's cause was such that George II was haunted by him in his dreams and would wake up screaming 'De gread Glenbogged is goming'.

The entrance to the castle building is in the east wall of the southwest tower, and it had an outer door and an inner yett. The door could not be opened until the yett behind had opened. A staircase led up from opposite this entrance to the first floor, where there was access to the spiral staircase in the cylindrical projection: the castle's staircases are supported by squinch-arches and not corbelling. The tower walls were equipped with gun loops all round. Glenbuchat remained in the hands of the Gordon family until the 18th century; the roof was taken off in the middle of the 19th century.

Some restoration work has been undertaken and much of the castle is still standing and has interesting carved stonework. Explore the first floor and the vaulted ground floor.

Location	Nr Strathdon, Aberdeenshire
Map ref	NJ 397148
Tel	01667 460232
Web	www.historic-scotland.gov.uk
Open	At all reasonable times

Hermitage

This brutal-looking tower-house castle, set against a backdrop of bleak moorland, was built over several centuries. Its position meant that it figured in many episodes of Scottish history and it changed hands several times, particularly during the Wars of Independence in the 13th and 14th centuries. For a time Hermitage was held by the wild and dangerous James Hepburn, Earl of Bothwell, whose liaison with Mary, Queen of Scots was the scandal of 16th-century Scotland.

History

The castle was begun in the early 13th century when Sir Nicholas de Soules put up a wooden fortress, which was captured in 1338 by the Knight of Liddesdale, Sir William Douglas. The 1st Earl of Douglas inherited Hermitage and built the original stone structure, a small rectangular enclosure, in the late 13th to early 14th centuries. Four great stone towers were added at the end of the 14th century: these are close together on the east and west sides and linked at the top by a continuous storey, giving the appearance of a huge stone wall with a great central pointed arch, reaching to the top storey from the ground. There were more alterations, notably the provision of wide-mouth gun ports in the 1540s.

The castle fell into disuse in the 1600s but its reputation as a forbidding ruin endured. Famously, Sir Walter Scott was painted with Hermitage Castle in the background in the 19th century. Although the exterior walls are largely intact, the interior is in a ruinous state. It is widely believed by local people that ghosts haunt the castle.

Location	Scottish Borders
Map ref	NY 497961
Tel	01387 372622
Web	www.historic-scotland.gov.uk
Open	Daily 9.30–6.30, Sun 2–6.30 Apr–Sep

Huntingtower

This tower house is made up from two separate rectangular tower blocks dating from the 15th century, joined by adding walling up to three storeys in the 17th century to form one building. Huntingtower, which was originally known as the House of Ruthven, is perhaps most famous as the scene of the Ruthven Raid of 1582 when William Ruthven, the Earl of Gowrie, and the Earl of Mar, kidnapped the boy-king James VI to get him away from the political and religious influence of their rivals, the Duke of Lennox and the Earl of Arran. For this treasonous act, William Ruthven was later executed.

The House of Ruthven was abolished after two later Ruthvens were disgraced. Its arms were deleted from the Book of Arms, hence the change of name to Huntingtower. The castle then passed to the Earls of Tuillibardine and the Earls of Atholl, who lived at Huntingtower until early in the 19th century.

The castle has exceptional 16th-century painted ceilings, uncovered during restoration work early in the 20th century.

Location	Perth, Perth & Kinross
Map ref	NO 082251
Tel	01738 627231
Web	www.historic-scotland.gov.uk
Open	Mon–Sun 9.30–6.30 Apr–Sep; Sat–Wed, 9.30–4.30 Oct–Mar

Huntly

Described as one of the noblest baronial ruins in Scotland this remarkable structure, a mixture of building periods, was the fortified residence of one of the wealthiest and most powerful families in Scotland, the Earls (and later Marquises) of Huntly.

The Earls of Huntly

There are the remains of three castles on the site at Huntly, the first was a motte castle built in the 12th century: the mound and some ditching are still there. Then a substantial L-plan tower was built in the bailey about the end of the 14th century, but only the foundations of this remain. The Gordon family owned Huntly Castle, and by the middle of the 15th century they were created the Earls of Huntly. The first earl, to reflect the family's new importance, built another, more palatial castle, the 'new werk', south of the L-plan, which was then much modified and altered and repaired during subsequent centuries, but the whole block is fascinating.

The basement is all that remains from the 15th century; the top floor has oriel windows which were put in very early in the 17th century. The façade above and below the oriel window line has an inscription bearing the name of the 5th Earl of Huntly, who by then had become the 1st Marquis of Huntly, and his wife. This earl had joined a revolt against James VI, had his home blown up and then, reconciled with the king, rebuilt it in an even grander style. By the time Huntly was held by government troops against the Jacobites in 1746 it had been abandoned and was falling into decay.

The ruins of this castle, which until *c.*1506 was known as the Peel of Strathbogie, remain an impressive testament to its former grandeur.

Location	Aberdeenshire
Map ref	NJ 532407
Tel	01466 793191
Web	www.historic-scotland.gov.uk
Open	Daily 9.30-6.30 Apr–Sep; Sat–Wed 9.30-4.30 Oct–Mar

Inverness

Only part of the curtain wall, a restored well and some earthworks remain of the first stone castle built here in the 12th century. It guarded routes to the Highlands. The castle was captured by the Lord of the Isles in 1491 but was retaken by James IV. It was severely damaged in Mary, Queen of Scots' reign, damaged again during the Civil War, and all but destroyed by the Young Pretender, Bonnie Prince Charlie, in 1746. A 19th-century neo-Norman castle, on the site, is a courthouse.

All that remains of the castle are parts of the curtain wall and some earthworks. The Drum Tower displays an exhibition on the castle's history.

Location	Highland
Map ref	NH 666451
Tel	01463 243363
Web	www.historic-scotland.gov.uk
Open	Daily 10.30–5.30 May–Sep

Kilchurn

Sited on a peninsula in Loch Awe, Kilchurn Castle stands as a splendid ruin among reeds and marshes. It began as a five-floor, square tower at the east, built in the middle of the 15th century by Colin Campbell of Glenorchy, 1st Earl of Breadalbane. Additions were made during the 16th century, and by the end of the 1600s, there were numerous buildings grouped round a courtyard. Kilchurn was abandoned in the middle of the 18th century and is now a gaunt shadow of its obvious former splendour. Access is by ferry or on foot; the castle is only open in the summer.

Location	Loch Awe, Argyll & Bute
Map ref	NN 133276
Tel	01866 833333 (Loch Awe boats)
Web	www.historic-scotland.gov.uk
Open	Daily 9.30–6.30 Apr–Sep

Kildrummy

A remarkable early 13th-century, red sandstone castle, Kildrummy was built by the Earl of Mar. A substantial D-shaped enclosure castle with a range of buildings was erected along the inner face of the northwest curtain surrounded by banks and ditches. Early in the 16th century the estate was handed to the Elphinstone family who added a tower house to the original construction, known as the Elphinstone Tower.

Kildrummy is now an impressive ruin but there is a model of how it looked in its heyday in the visitor centre.

Location	Nr Alford, Aberdeenshire
Map ref	NJ 455164
Tel	01975 571331
Web	www.historic-scotland.gov.uk
Open	Daily 9.30-6.30 Apr–Sep

Linlithgow

Sited on a mound overlooking Linlithgow Loch, this is the ruin of a great palace castle. It is roofless but has most of its walling, still showing its impressive size and architecture.

The basement and ground and first floors are accessible to visitors, as is Queen Margaret's Bower, high up and with views of the surrounding countryside. The fabric is of several building periods, from the 1400s to the 1600s.

A royal residence

Linlithgow may have begun as a royal manor house for Scottish kings, first of all for David I. The site fell into English hands in c.1300, and in 1302–3 an enclosure with turrets made of 'great logs not split too small' was erected on the mound by the order of Edward I and under the supervision of Master James of St George. The castle was besieged in 1303 but was not taken. After the Battle of Bannockburn, just over a decade later, the castle was returned to

the Scots and continued as a royal residence. In 1425, after a damaging fire, James I decided to build a fortified palace on the site and during the next decade more than £4,500 was spent.

The structure that emerged under the aegis of several kings was a fine mix of the best contemporary residential apartments and up-to-date fortifications. On the first floor of the eastern side is the 15th-century Lyon Chamber. The northern side of Linlithgow was reconstructed in the 1620s and the resulting Renaissance-style range is known as the New Wark. After the Union of the Crowns the Court moved to London. The palace, the birthplace of Mary, Queen of Scots, was damaged by fire in the 18th century and never restored.

Location	West Lothian
Map ref	NS 996774
Tel	01506 842896
Web	www.historic-scotland.gov.uk
Open	Daily 9.30–6.30; Apr–Sep; 9.30-4.30 Oct–Mar

Megginch

This late 15th-century L-plan tower house with gun-ports, built by the Hay family, became part of a larger and less fortified structure in the 18th century. The castle was used as a location for the 1990s film *Rob Roy*.

The gardens are renowned and include a fountain parterre, Gothic courtyard and a walled garden and water garden. Refreshments are available.

Location	Nr Perth, Perth & Kinross
Map ref	NO 242246
Tel	01821 642222
Web	www.scottishmuseums.org.uk
Open	Daily 2–5 Apr–Oct

Mey

The Castle of Mey, built in the 1560s was bought by Her Majesty Queen Elizabeth The Queen Mother in 1952, while in mourning after the death of her husband, King George VI. Falling for its isolated charm and hearing it was to be abandoned she decided to save it.

A passion for gardening

So began the Queen Mother's love affair with the Castle and Gardens of Mey. About 10km (6 miles) west of John o'Groats, it stands on rising ground near the seashore, overlooking the Pentland Firth and the Orkney Islands, a short journey from the port of Scrabster. Having acquired the most northerly castle on the British Isles, the Queen Mother restored it and created the beautiful gardens that can be seen today. For almost 50 years Her Majesty spent many happy summers at Mey.

Queen Mother's summer home

A tour allows a rare opportunity to enjoy the Queen Mother's summer home much as she left it after her last visit in October 2001. The tour passes through the principal rooms and some bedrooms, and includes the traditional Scottish walled garden (mostly planted with vegetables surrounded by fruit and herbaceous borders) and the East Garden created out of a wilderness by the Queen Mother.

In 1996 The Queen Mother created The Queen Elizabeth Castle of Mey Trust so that the castle could continue in perpetuity for the benefit of the people of Caithness.

Location	Thurso, Highland
Map ref	ND 290739
Tel	01847 851473
Web	www.castleofmey.org.uk
Open	Sat–Thu 10.30–4 mid-May–Sep. The castle and grounds are closed for the first 2 weeks in August

Ravenscraig

Ravenscraig was the first castle in Britain specifically planned for defence with guns. James II of Scotland, who initiated the work in 1460, intended it to be a coastal fortress to guard against any attack from the Firth of Forth. The castle is positioned on a prominent rocky site jutting into Kirkcaldy Bay. A wide, natural gully divides the site from the mainland, and this was artificially extended.

Two towers

There were two huge D-plan towers with 3–4.5m (10–15ft) thick walls. The western tower, whose outer wall stands sheer on a slope down to the beach, is in reality a great tower. It was fortified and residential with mural chambers on each floor, as well as main centre rooms with garderobes.

Both towers were given keyhole gun ports, some of them designed for falconets (small cannons) and the whole front of the castle presented a formidable array of gun ports through which the garrison could have discharged the most murderous fire.

The castle's position on the shore meant that, if it was beseiged, a garrison could hold out for a very long time because it could be supplied from the sea.

Ravenscraig was never finished; however, James II's widow, Mary of Gueldres, lived in the castle for a time after her husband's death, and the Sinclairs held it until the middle of the 17th century.

What to see

The castle, now in a park, overlooks the sea and the encroaching town. Where once it stood alone on the coast, the castle is no longer isolated. Ravenscraig has several decorative features, such as cable mouldings, armorial panels, gun loops and decorative stonework.

Location	Kirkaldy, Fife
Map ref	NT 290924
Tel	0131 6688800
Web	www.historic-scotland.gov.uk
Open	Open access

St Andrews

This interesting fortress stands on a rock promontory to the northeast of the city of St Andrews. The first stonework was erected late in the 12th century. Towards the end of the 14th century a major building programme began. This included erecting a curtain round the whole enclosure with two new towers and rebuilding the earlier fore tower.

St Andrews later became a favourite residence of royalty; James III was probably born there in 1451. The next phase of building was in the first half of the 16th century.

Siege tunnels

The castle was besieged in 1546–7 following the murder of Cardinal Beaton, Archbishop of St Andrews, by Protestant infiltrators. The Protestants captured the castle and held out for a year against the Catholic forces although extensive damage was inflicted on the castle. It finally fell into ruins after the Reformation.

During the siege the attackers sank a mine through the rock under the castle, tunnelling towards the fore tower. The defenders heard of this, calculated the tunnel's direction and sank a counter-mine, hoping to join up with the besiegers' tunnel and fight them The former, 2m (6ft) high and 1.5m (5ft) wide and slants down to pass under the ditch. The counter-mine is much the same size and it reached the head of the besiegers' mine nearly 12m (39ft) out from the fore tower where it was begun.

The mine and the counter-mine have survived to this day and visitors can walk (or crawl) through the tunnels. The visitor centre has interpretive displays.

Location	St Andrew's, Fife
Map ref	NO 513169
Tel	01334 477196
Web	www.historic-scotland.gov.uk
Open	Daily 9.30–6.30 Apr–Sep; 9.40–4.30 Oct–Mar

Smailholm Tower

A favourite castle of Sir Walter Scott, Smailholm Tower is a four-floor rectangular tower house standing on a rocky spur surrounded on three sides by cliffs and enclosed by a ditch and stone walling. The tower walls are almost 3m (10ft) thick and the tower reaches nearly 18.5m (60ft). The castle, which was built by the Pringle family in the 15th century, is now decayed and a fairly substantial ruin.

Visitors will be able to admire the surrounding areas from the top of the tower house. The castle has a display of costumed dolls and tapestries.

Location	Nr Kelso, Borders
Map ref	NT 638346
Tel	01573 460365
Web	wwww.historic-scotland.gov.uk
Open	Daily 9.30–6.30 Apr–Sep; Sat–Wed 9.30–4.30 Oct; Sat–Sun 9.30–4.30 Nov–Mar

Stirling

The landscape looks very different today but in medieval times marshes, hills and two rivers rendered Stirling Castle's towering rocky site highly defensible. With central Scotland's major route into the Highlands passing by this craggy site, control of Stirling Castle meant control of much of the country. Its strategic position led to its status as one of the most important fortresses in the kingdom and Stirling represented Scotland's resistance to English aggression in the Middle Ages.

By the time Alexander I died at the castle in 1124 Stirling was an important royal stronghold and later in the same century the fortress was one of the five castles surrendered to Henry II of England under the 1174 Treaty of Falaise, which made Scotland a feudal possession of England. The treaty was overturned by Richard I in 1189.

Won and lost

During the Scottish Wars of Independence Stirling Castle was often under attack, its buildings destroyed and then rebuilt. In 1296, it was seized by Edward I during his Scottish campaign: a year later, William Wallace recovered the castle after the Battle of Stirling Bridge but lost it again in 1298 when the Scottish were defeated at Falkirk. In 1299, the Scots took the fortress again and held

it until 1304, the year of the great siege by Edward I. By this time Stirling was the only noteworthy stronghold still under Scottish control and Edward planned his siege with care. For three months the garrison resisted everything Edward threw at it but eventually it surrendered. The English then held the castle for the next ten years, but in 1314 it was yielded to the Scots after their victory nearby at Bannockburn, and then dismantled.

A magnificent residence

The structure that endured so much battering began as a timber- and-earthwork castle. Nothing remains of Stirling's 12th- and 13th-century buildings, the complex that graces the huge rock stems from the 15th century and later. The great hall, the largest in Scotland – restored to all its medieval glory at the end of the 20th century – was one of the first and certainly the finest of the 15th-century Renaissance buildings erected anywhere in the British Isles.

Stirling was at the centre of the sumptuous court surrounding James IV and then his son, James V (who was crowned at Stirling in 1513, aged just 17 months, after his father's death at the Battle of Flodden). James V was responsible for the most outstanding building in the castle precincts, the magnificently façaded palace building, erected for James' second wife, Mary of Guise.

Abdication and rebellion

James and Mary's daughter was crowned Mary, Queen of Scots in the Chapel Royal at Stirling in September 1543 and her son, Prince James, was baptized at the castle in December 1566. Eight months later the castle saw the coronation of the 13-month-old infant after the forced abdication of his mother. James VI largely grew up at Stirling. When he succeeded to the English throne in 1603 James returned only once more, in 1617.

The fortress was strengthened between 1708 and 1714 during the Jacobite Rebellions. These new defences were tested in 1746 when 'Bonnie' Prince Charlie besieged the castle. This was Stirling's last experience of warfare although its military connections remained until 1964 as it became the base for the Argyll and Sutherland Highlanders whose regimental museum remains open to visitors in the Kings Old Building. The museum tells the story of the regiment from its foundation at the castle to the present day.

Attractions for the visitor

Restoration of the palace is under way, but the castle is still open to visitors.

Audio-visual tours help explain the history and development of the castle. There is a lot to see here and it is really a must for visitors to the area who can tour the rooms, halls, chapel, kitchens, courtyards, exhibitions and see the uniforms, medals, silver, paintings, colours and pipe banners on display at the Argyll and Sutherland Highlanders Regimental Museum.

The Chapel Royal displays two completed tapestries from The Hunt of the Unicorn series. A new Castle Exhibition, which has opened in the Queen Anne Casemates gives a detailed insight into the Stewart monarchy and its relevance to the castle's history. A café is open for refreshments and in summer you can sit outside on the café roof terrace and enjoy the views.

Left: At night Stirling Castle is dramatically floodlit.

Location	Stirling
Map ref	NS 788941
Tel	01786 450000
Web	www.historic-scotland.gov.uk
Open	Daily 9.30–6 Apr–Sep; 9.30–5 Oct–Mar

Tantallon

This is a fascinating and powerful castle on a coastal site. It sits on a promontory with three of its sides jutting into the Firth of Forth and below high, sheer rock cliffs falling straight down to the sea. On the fourth side, a ditch about 6m (20ft) wide is cut into the rock. Inside the ditch is a massive 15m (50ft) tall and 3.5m (10ft) thick battlemented curtain wall of dressed red freestone.

In the curtain is a central mid-tower containing the entrance and remains of end towers at the northwest and southeast. The ruins of all three towers rise to nearly 24.5m (83ft). The gatehouse tower had four floors of residential accommodation above the room that contained the portcullis mechanism and consisted at the front of a pair of square-plan wings up to the second floor.

This structure, together with a two-hall block at the north, dates from the 14th century when the castle was in the hands of William, 1st Earl of Douglas of the 'Black Douglas' family. Tantallon was attacked and bombarded by Cromwell's troops in 1651, and then it was abandoned.

Location	North Berwick, East Lothian
Map ref	NT 595850
Tel	01620 892727
Web	www.historic-scotland.gov.uk
Open	Daily 9.30–6.30 Apr–Sep; Sat–Wed 9.30–4.30 Oct–Mar

Threave

Threave stands on an islet in the River Dee and even as a ruin it is a mighty and forbidding structure. The massive great tower was partly enclosed by a powerful 'artillery' wall which had three cylindrical corner turrets.

Inspiring awe

Built by Archibald 'the Grim', 3rd Earl of Douglas, Lord of Galloway, in about 1370, Threave was a defensive structure as well as a building intended to impress. During the reign of James II the Earls of Douglas were locked in a deadly quarrel with the king who was determined to break their power.

In c.1454, defences were reinforced with the addition of the earliest 'artillery' wall in Britain along the sides of the castle that faced the mainland. The wall was 5.5m (18ft) tall and it was provided with vertical loops with embrasures for handguns and for crossbows: its towers were equipped with two types of gun-port, inverted keyholes and dumb-bells. Threave was besieged in 1455 by James II using the latest cannons and bombards, including the famous Mons Meg (now at Edinburgh Castle), and was eventually taken. It was slighted in the 17th century.

Visiting the castle

Today access to the islet is by taking a boat that departs from the small jetty standing nearby. The property is closed in winter. There is a walk of about 2km (1 mile) to the castle from the boat. You will find a tea room next to the car park.

Location	Nr Castle Douglas, Dumfries & Galloway
Map ref	NX 739623
Tel	07711 223101
Web	www.historic-scotland.gov.uk
Open	Daily 9.30–6.30 Apr–Sep

Tolquhon

A Preston and then a Forbes family castle, the substantial ruins of Tolquhon derive from two main periods, the late 15th century and between 1584 and 1589. The first period saw the construction of the 'auld tour' (old tower), but only the vaulted basement and parts of the first floor of this remain.

In 1584, William Forbes enlarged the castle round the old tower. He constructed a substantial irregular quadrangular enclosure with ranges of buildings along the inside of three of its walls. Then he added two further towers, both equipped with gun ports. The parapet of the 'auld tour' was machicolated. The castle was abandoned at the end of the 19th century. The remains of the buildings are substantial and merit a visit.

Location	Tarves, Aberdeenshire
Map ref	NJ 872286
Tel	01651 851286
Web	www.historic-scotland.gov.uk
Open	Open daily 9.30–6.30 Apr–Sep; 9.30–4.30 Oct–Nov. Last entry 30 mins before closing

Urquhart

U rquhart was a substantial enclosure castle built on the site of a motte castle. It was one of Scotland's largest castles.

Structure of the castle

On a sandstone promontory on the shores of Loch Ness, the enclosure was defended from the landward side by a wide, deep ditch that was crossed by a bridge with high walls on either side and was broken in the middle by a drawbridge. The bridge led out from a massive twin cylindrical-towered gatehouse in the high stone curtain. This curtain survives in part.

At the northeast end of the enclosure is the ruined shell of the great tower whose basement dates from the 14th century. The next storeys are 16th century (probably rebuilding of older work) and the top is 17th century. Gun-ports were inserted in the 16th century. South of the great tower is a range of ruined buildings which once contained the great chamber, hall and kitchen and at the end of this range, an inlet for the loch water, a landing place and a sea gate.

The castle has had a turbulent past. By 1297 Edward I of England had Urquhart under his control. It was retaken by the Scots in 1303, changed hands twice more, and in 1313 became the property of Randolph, Earl of Moray, one of Bruce's greatest friends and counsellors.

Visiting

This popular castle has an excellent visitor centre with audio-visual displays and a model of the intact castle. There is much to explore at this evocative site.

Location	Drumnadrochit, Highland
Map ref	NH 531286
Tel	01456 450551
Web	www.historic-scotland.gov.uk
Open	Daily 9.30–6.30 Apr–Sep; 9.30–4.30 Oct–Mar

Wales

For the Normans, Wales was a land of two parts: the lowlands and hills of the south, and the wild, untameable mountain lands of the north. They came to the south early, and claimed much of it, building castles as they went. The Welsh retreated to the hills and mountains and fought on until Edward I built his 'iron ring' of castles in the north at the end of the 13th century.

Widespread open revolt against English rule began again under the 15th-century campaign of Owain Glyn Dwr. Castles were a central focus of this rebellion, but Owain's own castle headquarters at Sycarth is now a forgotten, inaccessible tree-covered mound.

The legacy of castles in Wales is tremendously rich, with many evocative ruins in outstanding landscape settings.

Beaumaris

The ultimate in concentric castles, Beaumaris is the last of the fortresses built by Edward I. Started in 1295, it cost nearly £15,000 and took over 35 years to build, but it was never completed. At the peak of building, more than 2,500 people were working on the castle.

The master builder

Edward I commissioned Master James of St George to build the fortress shortly after an uprising by Madog ap Llywelyn. Edward brought James over from Europe: he had already been involved with the construction of several of the king's great castles in Wales. Beaumaris, his final work in Wales,

is considered by many to be the finest of all the Edwardian castles, and one of the most technically perfect in all Britain.

At Beaumaris James of St George oversaw the building of two perfectly symmetrical rings of walling with flanking towers and gatehouses surrounded by a broad wet moat fed by the tidal waters of the Menai Strait. A dock in the outer ring enabled seagoing supply vessels to unload their cargoes directly into the castle.

An unfinished project

The outer ring of walls, about half as thick as the walls of the inner ward, were built to an octagonal plan with cylindrical flanking turrets. Inside these, the 5m (16ft) thick walls of the

inner ward were built to a square plan with six towers and two vast gatehouses. Both keep-like gatehouses were intended to contain opulent residential suites and to be the strongest parts of the castle. None of the towers or gatehouses was completed to full height.

Despite grand intentions for Beaumaris, the initial flurry of construction lasted only about three years until 1298 when funds dried up. Small-scale building resumed again early in the 14th century but within 20 years Beaumaris was deteriorating. Edward's plans for Beaumaris were never fulfilled but his legacy here is powerful enough to have earned the castle World Heritage inscribed status.

Exploring

This is a thoroughly satisfying castle to explore although finding your way around can be bewildering, but you are rewarded with an insight into the power and authority conveyed by the structure. The views of the Menai Straits from the castle are also wonderful.

Location	Isle of Anglesey
Map ref	SH 607763
Tel	01248 810361
Web	www.cadw.wales.gov.uk
Open	Daily 9.30–5 Apr–May & Oct; 9.30–6 Jun–Sep; Mon–Sat 9.30–4, Sun 11–4 Nov–Mar

Caerphilly

This was the first concentric castle built from scratch in Britain. Its blend of land and water defences represented the highest sophistication in military architecture at the time of its construction. Despite sieges and long periods of neglect much of the castle has survived and it is now a spectacular ruin.

Earl Gilbert de Clare began the castle in 1268 and it was completed quite quickly.

Hugh Despenser

In 1316 Caerphilly was attacked during a Welsh uprising, but sustained little damage. The following year, the castle came to Edward II's favourite, Hugh Despenser the younger, who rebuilt the great hall in the 1320s. The castle was threatened again in the winter of 1326 when the forces of Isabella, the estranged wife of Edward II, laid siege to the fortress where the king had earlier taken refuge and left much royal treasure. Caerphilly began to fall into disrepair later in the 14th century, but was extensively restored in the early 1930s by the 4th Marquess of Bute. Today, it is one of Britain's most outstanding 13th-century castles.

What to see

On the south dam platform, once a tournament field, are working replica siege engines. Look out too for the leaning tower, a victim of subsidence, listing at a greater angle than the Tower of Pisa.

There are exhibitions, and spiral stairs reach those that are housed in the towers. Information panels are displayed in the castle.

Location	Caerphilly
Map ref	ST 155870
Tel	029 2088 3143
Web	www.cadw.wales.gov.uk
Open	Daily 9.30–5 Apr–May & Oct; 9.30–6 Jun–Sep; Mon–Sat 9.30–4, Sun 11–4 Nov–Mar

Caldicot

Caldicot began as a motte castle with two baileys, built beside a stream, probably in the 11th century. The present castle was erected by the Earl of Hereford. It developed from the early 13th century into a large, stirrup-shaped stone enclosure with high walls, flanking towers, an unusual gatehouse and a cylindrical great tower erected on the motte in one corner. It stands on a splayed plinth and has a mural staircase to the basement and a spiral staircase up to the second floor.

More building took place during the next century and includes the 14th-century gatehouse. This is rectangular with square turrets at each end and – since it intended to be a residential structure – handsome accommodation. The castle was bought and restored as a family home in the middle of the 19th century.

Attractions for the visitor

The restoration made it even more picturesque and today the castle is the excellent focal point of a 22ha (55-acre) country park. A self-guided cassette tour provides visitors with a complete story of the castle. A large number of events take place throughout the summer, with many especially for children and the rare plants fair and Roman Britain re-enactment will appeal to visitors of all ages. There is a tea room for refreshments if required.

Location	Monmouthshire
Map ref	ST 487885
Tel	01291 420241
Web	www.caldicotcastle.co.uk
Open	Daily 11–5 Mar–Oct; Sat–Sun 11–4 Nov–Feb. Please visit website or telephone for winter school holiday closures. After October 2006, winter hours might change – please contact the castle for information

Cardiff

Cardiff began as a motte castle, raised in about 1080 on the site of a Roman fort. In the 12th century a 12-sided shell enclosure was erected on the motte with a tower-like projection on one side.

The Black Tower

Medieval additions include the Black Tower built in the 1200s below the motte and connected to it by a wing wall, an octagonal tower, c.1420s, on the south side of the shell enclosure and a substantial gatehouse linked to the Black Tower by a wall across the bailey. Later apartments in the bailey included a range against the western wall, substantially remodelled in the 18th and 19th centuries.

Powerful families

Cardiff is a good example of how an earth-and-timber motte castle was converted to a stone fortress. It has belonged to some powerful families, including the de Clares and, in the 14th century, the Despensers. The castle was held by the Royalists for most of the Civil War. In the 19th century, the 3rd Marquess of Bute employed architect William Burges to remodel it in the Gothic Revival style.

A splendid place to visit

There are two military museums, and visitors will enjoy the magnificent Mediterranean gardens and the castle's grounds, with their peacocks, ducks and geese. For refreshments there is a tea room. Regular events take place throughout the year.

Location	Cardiff
Map ref	ST 180767
Tel	029 2087 8100
Web	www.cardiffcastle.com
Open	Daily 9.30–6 Mar–Oct; 9.30–5 Nov–Feb. Last entry and last tour 1 hour before closing

Carew

Carew stands on a rock above the shore overlooking a rare tidal mill where the River Carew enters the sea. It began as an earthwork castle early in the 12th century. Later that century the original gatehouse was altered to make a tower, and later still, a square-plan curtain wall was built round the tower. The curtain had four large flanking towers of various shapes, two of which were cylindrical on spur bases.

Late in the 13th century an outer ward with its own gatehouse into the main enclosure was added. This enclosure was altered in the 14th and 15th centuries when a great hall and imposing porch were built, thus converting the castle into a grand mansion. There were further alterations in the 16th century. Carew was badly damaged in the Civil War, and by 1685 it had been abandoned.

The setting, and nearby tidal mill (one of only four that have been restored in Britain) and beautiful Carew Cross, make this an excellent place to visit.

Location	Pembrokeshire
Map ref	SN 045037
Tel	01646 651782
Web	www.carewcastle.com
Open	Daily 10–5 Apr–Oct. Tours of the castle (no additional charge) are available at 2.30 each day

Caernarfon

Caernarfon, part of Edward I's defensive ring of castles, was intended as a powerful symbol of the conquest of Wales. The castle was never finished but it was the grandest of Edward's Welsh structures. Edward's son, the first English prince of Wales and the future Edward II, was born there in 1284.

Strategic importance

The position of Caernarfon, on the banks of the River Seiont where it flows into the Menai Strait, was strategically important. The site of the Roman fort of Segontium lay only a short distance away, and Edward raised his castle on the spot where Hugh of Avranches had erected a motte and bailey c.1090. Building began in 1283, overseen by Master James of St George: this included the huge polygonal Eagle Tower.

The castle was taken in 1294 during the revolt of Madog ap Llywelyn but was regained by the English in 1295 when work resumed on the unfinished defences, including the mighty twin-towered King's Gate. Although Edward's attention eventually turned to Scotland, building work at Caernarfon continued until 1330, but was never completed.

Caernarfon lost its defensive and administrative importance after the Act of Union in the 16th century.

Attractions for the visitor

The castle, along with the town walls, is a World Heritage Site. It is packed with interest and there is much to explore, including a military museum. The covered passageways and wall-walks will fuel your imagination of castle life in Edward I's time, and the exhibitions and displays will fill in any gaps in Caernarfon's history.

The regimental museum covers the history of the Royal Welch Fusiliers with exhibitions and interactive displays. In addition, the castle hosts several events throughout the year.

Location	Gwynedd
Map ref	SH 477626
Tel	01286 677617
Web	www.cadw.wales.gov.uk
Open	Daily 9.30–5 Apr–May & Oct; 9.30–6 Jun–Sep; Mon–Sat 9.30–4, Sun 11–4 Nov–Mar

Carreg Cennen

Location	Nr Llandeilo, Carmarthenshire
Map ref	SN 668191
Tel	01588 822291
Web	www.cadw.wales.gov.uk
Open	Daily 9.30-6.30 Apr–Oct; 9.30-dusk Nov–Mar

This powerful courtyard castle stands on a 91.5m (300ft) high limestone crag overlooking the Cennen valley. Although preceded by an earlier castle, the existing stronghold was begun in the late 13th century.

History of the castle

The inner ward, which is entered via an elaborate barbican and a strong gatehouse, has a long range incorporating the hall and other domestic buildings along the east wall. A covered gallery along the cliffside leads to a 'secret' cave that may have contained a source of fresh water.

Carreg Cennen is very much a ruin, but its layout and sophisticated defences are clear. It was severely damaged by Owain Glyn Dwr early in the 15th century. After repair during the reign of Henry V, it was a stronghold during the Wars of the Roses, but was finally rendered useless as a castle by the Yorkists after their victory at Mortimer's Cross in 1461.

Visiting

This is one of the most beautifully set of all Welsh castles, with truly breathtaking views of Black Mountain across the valley from the parapets. Reaching the hilltop requires a somewhat invigorating climb, which may not be suitable for elderly people, but is well worth the effort for the more able-bodied.

Castell-y-Bere

This Welsh-built castle was raised on a spur below Cader Idris, and resembles the medieval German hill castles such as Staufen. It was probably begun in 1221 by Llywelyn the Great (c.1196–1240), and comprised an irregular curtained enclosure with a D-shaped tower at the northern end and a rectangular, keep-like tower to the south.

The entrance to the castle was defended with two gate-towers, each equipped with a drawbridge, and overlooked by a nearby round tower on the curtain wall. Llywelyn the Great, or perhaps his grandson, Llywelyn ap Gruffydd (d. 1282), built another D-shaped tower, but it stood isolated a short distance south of the main enclosure.

Although the castle was formidable because of its position, it surrendered to Edward I's men after a short siege in 1283. The English strengthened Castell-y-Bere with walls linking the isolated southern tower to the main part of the castle, but the stronghold was besieged again in 1294, during the revolt of Madog ap Llywelyn. The outcome of the siege is unknown, but occupation of the castle ceased around the end of the 13th century.

The remains are very ruinous, but impressive.

Location	Abergynolwyn, Gwynedd
Map ref	SH 667086
Tel	01443 336 000
Open	At all reasonable times

Chepstow

Domesday Book records show that it was William FitzOsbern, Earl of Hereford who established the castle of Estriguil, or Chepstow, on the limestone cliffs towering above the River Wye. FitzOsbern has also been credited with the construction of the great tower – a substantial quadrilateral two-storey building, about 30.5 x 12m (100 x 40ft), standing on a splayed plinth – giving rise to the claim that it represents the earliest stone keep in Britain. A recent re-evaluation of the castle, however, suggests that William the Conqueror is a more likely candidate for builder of the great tower. Chepstow was in royal hands after 1075 and the king may have planned the tower, which has few domestic facilities or defensive features, as a great audience chamber where he could assert his regal authority in Wales.

Modernizing

William Marshal, one of the greatest knights of his age and later Earl of Pembroke (1199–1219), obtained Chepstow by marriage in 1189, and soon set about modernizing the castle, which had probably changed little during the 12th century. Work on the defences of the lower bailey was underway in the 1190s, and the design of the gatehouse, with two cylindrical towers flanking the gate-passage, was ahead of its time. Marshal also provided the middle bailey with a curtain wall with rounded mural towers, and rebuilt and strengthened the defences of the existing Norman upper bailey.

After his death, five of William Marshal's sons held the castle in succession between 1219 and 1245. During that time, the great tower was remodelled and another storey was added at its west end. An upper barbican was added to bolster defences at the western end.

Marten's Tower

Roger Bigod, 5th earl of Norfolk (1270–1306), completed the upper storey of the great tower,

and built a sumptuous new domestic range in the lower bailey. He also added a huge D-shaped mural tower (19m/63ft) at the south-east corner of the lower bailey. It is known as Marten's Tower because Henry Marten, a signatory to the death warrant of Charles I, was imprisoned there after the Restoration of Charles II.

Chepstow overlooked a harbour on the River Wye, which meant the castle could be provisioned by ships coming from Bristol. Never attacked in the Middle Ages, the castle was besieged twice in the Civil War as a Royalist stronghold. Much renovation was undertaken in the 17th century to equip the castle for guns and musketry.

Visitors

The ruins stretch magnificently along the Wye, with the Norman great tower still standing at the heart of the castle. Exhibitions are displayed in the castle today.

Location	Monmouthshire
Map ref	ST 533941
Tel	01291 624065
Web	www.cadw.wales.gov.uk
Open	Daily 9.30–5 Apr–May & Oct; 9.30–6 Jun–Sep; Mon–Sat 9.30–4, Sun 11–4 Nov–Mar

Chirk

In the 1280s the Mortimer family began a lordship castle here with a view across Cheshire towards the Pennines. The fortress became a quadrangle with squat but substantial cylindrical corner towers and half-round towers, which remain in the present mansion. It is thought that the work went on into the 1320s when Roger Mortimer was disgraced and put to death. In 1595 the castle was sold to Thomas Myddleton who remodelled it; his descendants still live here. Chirk was besieged in the Civil War but was surrendered to prevent destruction.

Visitor attractions

The castle, gardens and parkland, in the care of the National Trust, are open in summer.

The castle's interior is magnificent, with sumptuous furnishings and decoration that reflect the changing styles over Chirk's 700-year history. Visitors can see the fine tapestries on display, and the medieval dungeon, as well as the magnificent wrought-iron gates. A tea room provides refreshments.

Location	Wrexham
Map ref	SJ 275388
Tel	01691 777701
Web	www.nationaltrust.org.uk
Open	Castle Wed–Sun 12–5 mid-Mar to Sep; Wed–Sun 12–4 Oct. Gardens Wed–Sun 11–6 mid-Mar to Sep; Wed–Sun 11–5 Oct

Cilgerran

Built on a rocky promontory of great natural strength overlooking the Teifi Gorge, with rock-cut ditches at the south end, Cilgerran probably began as a Norman enclosure castle with an outer bailey early in the 12th century.

Expansion and rebuilding

In 1223, William Marshal the younger began a major rebuilding of the castle by inserting the cylindrical east tower into the circuit of the Norman enclosure. During the next two decades, William and his brothers, who succeeded him as lords of Cilgerran, constructed the masonry defences of the outer ward and added the imposing west tower and a strong gatehouse to the inner ward.

By the 1320s the castle was ruinous. To counter a threatened French invasion, Edward III ordered repairs in 1377 and the north tower and various domestic buildings were raised in the inner war. Cilgerran was attacked during the Owain Glyn Dwr's uprising in the early 1400s, and may have been briefly held by

the rebels; records indicate that considerable damage was done to the castle.

The castle's surviving features include the mighty twin round towers and the curtain wall.

Location	Ceredigion
Map ref	SN 195431
Tel	01239 615007
Web	www.cadw.wales.gov.uk
Open	Daily 9.30–6.30 Apr–Oct; 9.30–dusk Nov–Mar

BUILDING CASTLES

CASTLES SUCH AS THOSE SHOWN ON THE BAYEUX TAPESTRY COULD BE BUILT IN A FEW DAYS. SOME OF EDWARD I'S 13TH-CENTURY CASTLES IN WALES REMAINED UNFINISHED YEARS AFTER THEY WERE BEGUN, AND BEAUMARIS WAS NEVER COMPLETED. BUILDING CASTLES BECAME MORE COMPLEX AS THE REQUIREMENTS OF THEIR OWNERS CHANGED.

When the Normans first arrived their priority was to dominate and to make sure rebellion was kept down as much as possible. Motte and bailey castles were a perfect solution in many ways: quick to build, they could be thrown up using materials found on the spot.

As stone replaced wood and earth, castle building became more expensive and time-consuming, especially when prestigious castles were involved. Here, the owners wanted to show not only that they had power and strength, but that they had both taste and wealth.

For example, Caen stone from Normandy was considered to be not only the right quality for castles, but it was also lovely to look at, so it was imported at great expense. As castles became ever more sophisticated, so they required greater and wider building skills and increasingly more workers.

Harlech, one of Edward I's great strongholds in Wales, had a workforce of 546 labourers, 227 masons and 115 quarrymen, not to mention smiths, carpenters and other highly skilled

workers. Even so, this stage of the work took seven years, and at an enormous cost. Records show that most of the workers came from England. But with some coming from as far away as the southwest the local economies must have been deeply affected as the demand for foodstuffs and raw materials grew.

Medieval castle builders had limited technologies to call on, but they used scaffolding in the same way that we do today, except that their poles were made of wood. Their skills are not in doubt, since so many castles survive today, albeit in ruined condition. Such ruins are often not the fault of weathering or natural causes but of deliberate destruction, or slighting. Castles frequently changed hands, and if this happened after a siege, it was often the case that the besiegers would attempt to make the castle incapable of being defended again.

Since castle walls could be several metres/feet thick at their base, destroying them could be very time-consuming, as the demolishers of such castles as Corfe found to their cost. It took them weeks!

Conwy

One of Edward I's second tranche of castles in Wales, Conwy's construction was overseen by the Master of the King's Works in Wales, James of St George. Work began in 1283 and proceeded quickly, so the castle was virtually complete by 1287. The bill came to nearly £20,000, the biggest sum spent on any castle in Wales between 1277 and 1304. At the end of it, Edward I was presented with an almost perfect structure, the most compact agglomerate of turretry in the British Isles.

Strength, terror, dominion

Tailored to fit the rock site chosen for guarding the entrance to the River Conwy, the castle was a vast enclosure divided into an inner and an outer ward, separated by a thick wall with, at each end, one of the eight flanking towers. The towers themselves are massive, over 21.5m (70ft) tall, well over 10m (33ft) in diameter with walls up to 4m (13ft) thick, and they have several storeys equipped with rooms and staircases. The castle was part of an impressive walled town with its circuit of walls guarded by 21 towers and three twin-towered gatehouse, and the entire massive construction represented all that Edward I stood for – strength, terror, dominion and permanence.

Decay

The Welsh hated the castle, yet it was not besieged until the Civil War. Conwy was used sporadically during the 14th century and then began to decay over the years. In 1609 it was described as 'utterly decayed' and after its slighting it was left as an impressive shell.

For visitors

This extraordinary building is a World Heritage Site and one of Britain's most impressive ruins. Don't miss the opportunity to walk the town walls, the most complete surviving such fortifications in Europe.

Location	Conwy
Map ref	SH 783774
Tel	01492 592358
Web	www.cadw.wales.gov.uk
Open	Daily 9.30–5 Apr–May & Oct; 9.30–6 Jun–Sep; Mon–Sat 9.30–4, Sun 11–4 Nov–Mar

Criccieth

In the decade before his death in 1240, Llywelyn the Great established Criccieth on a high peninsula in the northeast corner of Cardigan Bay. The site was naturally strong, with impressive sea cliff defences, and further strengthened with ditches and banks. Llywelyn erected a pentagonal enclosure with a rectangular tower to the southeast and an impressive twin-towered gatehouse overlooking the approach from vulnerable landward side.

Llywelyn ap Gruffudd (d. 1282) added the outer ward with substantial rectangulars towers to the southwest and north and a south-facing outer gatehouse. Substantial works, which may have included the remodelling of the towers and the construction of new buildings within the castle, were undertaken during the reigns of Edward I and Edward II. Criccieth was captured by Owain Glyn Dwr in 1404, and appears to have been burned.

A splendid seaside setting makes the site well worth a visit but note that there is a steep climb up to the entrance.

Location	Gwynedd
Map ref	SH 500377
Tel	01766 522227
Web	www.cadw.wales.gov.uk
Open	Daily 10–5 Apr–May, Oct; 10–6 Jun–Sep; Mon–Sat 9.30–4, Sun 11–4 Nov–Mar

Dolbadarn

From its boomerang-shaped platform between the Peris and Padarn lakes, Dolbadarn Castle commanded the entrance to the Llanberis Pass. The east side is protected by steep slopes above the Peris and the gentler approach from the west is covered by two towers. The cylindrical great tower, sitting astride the curtain round the site, is of slate and grit rubble. Its walls are 2–2.5m (7–8ft) thick and contain a spiral staircase. The height once reached nearly 15m (50ft).

Erected by Llywelyn the Great, Dolbadarn took shape in three phases of construction during the period between the second and fourth decades of the 13th century. It lost its strategic significance after the Edwardian conquest of Wales and was partially dismantled, but it continued in use as the centre of a royal manor.

Location	Nr Llanberis, Gwynedd
Map ref	SH 586598
Tel	01443 336000
Web	www.cadw.wales.gov.uk
Open	Open access

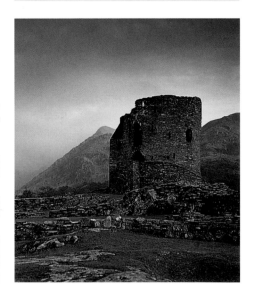

Flint

Flint was the first of the Edwardian castles to be begun in North Wales during the king's campaign of 1277. It was planned, like Rhuddlan, to be associated with a fortified town near by and, also like Rhuddlan, was given direct access to tidal waters for easy delivery of supplies by water.

The great tower

The roughly rectangular stone enclosure has three substantial cylindrical corner towers and, on the fourth corner, separated by its own moat, was a huge great tower protected by the River Dee. The cylindrical great tower was the dominating feature and it was designed to a unique plan; above a basement stood two, or perhaps three, storeys, each with ring of wedge-shaped mural chambers surrounding a central circular shaft. The mural chambers included a chapel, kitchen, garderobes and residential rooms. Construction was spread mainly over the years 1277–86 and cost about £7,000.

In 1399 Henry Bolingbroke (soon to be Henry IV) captured Richard II at Flint before forcing him to return to London and abdicate. During the Civil War the castle changed hands several times, surrendering finally to Parliament in 1646.

Visiting

Flint was slighted so thoroughly that, according to an eyewitness writing six years later, it was 'almost buried in its own ruins'. There is, however, enough left to see the general plan of the castle and the cylindrical great tower and to explore the remnants of buildings and walkways.

Location	Flintshire
Map ref	SJ 247733
Tel	01443 336000
Web	www.cadw.wales.gov.uk
Open	Open access at reasonable times

Grosmont

Grosmont is an interesting castle built on a main border route between Wales and England. The compact masonry enclosure is on the large mound of its Norman earth-and-timber precursor, encircled by a deep ditch. Grosmont consists of a compact enclosure of stone surrounded by a moat which contained a rectangular hall tower, a gatehouse building at the southeast corner and a rectangular building with a D-ended tower at its west end. A stone curtain with two semi-cylindrical flanking towers completed the enclosure.

History

The earliest surviving structure is the hall tower, built in the opening years of the 13th century by Hubert de Burgh, who held the 'Three Castles' of Grosmont, Skenfrith, and White Castle at Llantilio. The erection of the hall tower swept away a section of the existing timber defences, and, between about 1219 and 1232, Hubert replaced the rest with a stone curtain wall with three round mural towers and, in the southeast corner, a gatehouse abutting the hall tower

Further building work took place in the 14th century when the castle was held by the house of Lancaster. The northernmost of de Burgh's mural towers was demolished to ground level to make way for two rectangular blocks of apartments, and other parts of the castle were remodelled. Grosmont was attacked by Owain Glyn Dwr in 1404–5 but the Welsh attackers were defeated as reinforcements arrived. Grosmont was ruinous by the 16th century.

Today the ruins are accessed via a wooden walkway over the moat.

Location	Nr Abergavenny, Monmouthshire
Map ref	SO 405244
Tel	01443 336000
Web	www.cadw.wales.gov.uk
Open	Open access at reasonable times

Harlech

The second phase of Edward I's fortress-construction programme in Wales in the 1280s embraced four of the biggest castles in Britain – Beaumaris, Caernarfon, Conwy and Harlech.

A splendid construction

One of the two concentric castles, Harlech, was completed between 1283–90. Master James of St George directed its building and from 1290–93 he was its constable, a post that enhanced his status while he continued to act as Master of the King's Works in Wales.

The design of Harlech was simple yet immensely formidable: the dominant structure is the gatehouse, a massive, oblong structure like a great tower with three storeys and, at the front, flanking twin cylindrical towers. The upper storeys of the gatehouse contained fine residential apartments, which were reached by staircases in small cylindrical towers placed at the corners of the gatehouse's inner face. A wide external stair also gave direct access to the first floor from the inner ward.

History

Harlech's impregnability was tested in 1294, when it was attacked by Welsh patriots led by Prince Madog ap Llywelyn – just 37 men beat off the assault. However, Owain Glyn Dwr had more success when he besieged the castle in 1404. Harlech was the last Royalist stronghold to fall during the Civil War and when it fell the Royalist cause was lost and the Parliamentary forces slighted it.

For visitors

This World Heritage Site is well worth a visit for its superb architecture and setting, best appreciated from the wall-walk which gives tremendous views. The castle offers a wide variety of events and theatre performances are also staged regularly.

Location	Gwynedd
Map ref	SH 581312
Tel	01766 780552
Web	www.cadw.wales.gov.uk
Open	Daily 9.30–5 Apr–May & Oct; 9.30–6 Jun–Sep; Mon–Sat 9.30–4, Sun 11–4 Nov–Mar

Kidwelly

The striking ruins of Kidwelly Castle stand on a bluff beside the River Gwendraeth. The castle began as a large Norman ringwork of c.1106. A deep curving ditch defined the D-shaped site, with the straight, eastern, side protected by the steep slope to the river.

History

The outer curtain wall preserves evidence indicating that the first moves to replace the earth-and-timber fortifications with stone were probably made in the late 12th or early 13th century. However, much of the credit for the great stronghold that now stands must go to the de Chaworth brothers, Payn and Patrick, who transformed Kidwelly into a concentric castle in the 1270s and early 1280s. They built a square inner ward with cylindrical towers on the four corners, and rebuilt the outer curtain with four half-cylindrical mural towers and a gatehouse to the north and, presumably, to the south. In c.1300, the fine chapel tower, supported on a spur base and built into the slope of the bluff, was added, along with domestic buildings in the inner ward. The

substantial south gatehouse was begun at the end of the 14th century and not completed until 1422. It had three storeys and spacious accommodation, probably for the constable. By then Kidwelly was an administrative centre for the Duchy of Lancaster. The castle withstood an attack in 1403 by Owain Glyn Dwr.

Visiting

Today, there is a site exhibition and audio tours guide visitors around this splendid castle, one of the best preserved in Carmarthenshire.

Location	Carmarthenshire
Map ref	SN 409701
Tel	01554 890104
Web	www.cadw.wales.gov.uk
Open	Daily 9.30–5 Apr–May & Oct; 9.30–6 Jun–Sep; Mon–Sat 9.30–4, Sun 11–4 Nov–Mar

Laugharne

A castle was built here in the 12th century. Later, in the mid-13th century, Guy de Brian IV reconstructed the inner ward of castle, placing a cylindrical great tower and another circular tower astride the curtain wall. His successor, another Guy, added the inner gatehouse and improved the defences of the outer ward. The inner ward was converted to a mansion in the 16th century by Sir John Perrott, also the owner of Carew Castle. During the Civil War, Laugharne was held by the Royalists but fell to Parliament and was slighted. In the 18th century, the castle grounds were landscaped and turned into a garden.

Dylan Thomas

The ruins, in a beautiful setting by the River Taf estuary, have recently been restored, as have the Victorian gardens. Laugharne has a link with Dylan Thomas who lived and worked there near the castle from 1949 to 1953.

Location	Carmarthenshire
Map ref	SN302107
Tel	01994 427906
Web	www.cadw.wales.gov.uk
Open	Daily 10–5 Apr–Sep

Llansteffan

Llansteffan was an imposing double enclosure castle and its ruins make a dramatic gesture standing high above the golden sandy beaches of the coast below. The promontory upon which the Normans founded the castle had been the site of an Iron Age hill fort. A double ditch protected the castle on the west, while steeply sloping ground provided strong natural defences on the other three sides.

History

The inner enclosure, shaped like an irregular polygon, was the first part of the castle to have its earth-and-timber defences replaced in stone. Its masonry curtain wall was raised in the late 12th century, and a round mural tower and gatehouse were added in the early to mid-13th century.

The outer enclosure was fortified in the 13th century with a stone curtain, flanking towers and a bastion at the eastern corner. Late in the 13th century, the great gatehouse was erected

on the north side and much of it stands today. It was turned into a grand residence in the last years of the 15th century.

The castle was frequently attacked and sometimes held by the Welsh, but for much of the Middle Ages it was in the hands of the de Camvilles. It briefly fell to the Welsh during the revolt of Owain Glyn Dwr in the early 15th century. In later years it became a farmyard.

For visitors

Access to the castle is along a steep, fairly uneven path. The wide, sandy beach below will please children, but unfortunately swimming is not permitted.

Location	Carmarthenshire
Map ref	SN 352102
Tel	01443 336000
Web	www.cadw.wales.gov.uk
Open	Open access at reasonable times

Manorbier

This was the birthplace in 1146 of Giraldus Cambrensis (Gerald of Wales), the celebrated Welsh scholar and chronicler who served Henry II, Richard I and John. The castle began as an earthwork of the late 11th century, and in the 12th century it received a square three-storeyed great tower. Other stone buildings were added, including a hall block, and by the 13th century it consisted of two high stone curtain enclosures in line, with flanking towers (cylindrical in the case of the outer enclosure) and with a strong square gatehouse. Giraldus described the castle as 'excellently well defended by turrets and bulwarks'. Manorbier's residential features were manifest, notably the state apartments in the inner enclosure, the fishpond and the park.

Visiting the castle

The castle is superbly sited on the beautiful Pembrokeshire coast, and thanks to a relatively peaceful history and the attentions of a 19th-century tenant, is in a good state of repair. Exhibitions are held throughout the year in the keep, and there are audio-visual displays and guided tours. A tea room is open for refreshments.

Location	Nr Tenby, Pembrokeshire
Map ref	SS 064978
Tel	01834 871394
Open	Daily 10.30–5.30 Easter–Sep

Newcastle

A stone enclosure of the mid- to late 12th century was raised here on a steep spur overlooking the River Ogmore, probably upon the site of an earthwork castle of c.1106. The plan is polygonal with nine unequal sides and two almost square-plan towers in the curtain, one at the west angle, one at the south. The second tower was residential (with fireplaces, windows, staircases) and rose to three storeys. Further buildings were also residential; the footings of a detached structure lie to the north, and the foundations of two halls are against the east curtain wall. The entrance to the enclosure was adjacent to the south tower, through an decorated round-headed arch.

Location	Bridgend
Map ref	SS 902801
Tel	01443 336000
Web	www.cadw.wales.gov.uk
Open	Access at reasonable times

Old Beaupre

An Elizabethan quadrangular mansion, which incorporates stonework of a late 13th- to early 14th-century structure. The medieval remains include a gatehouse, which may have led to other buildings now vanished. There are other segments of the same wing, which are now part of the Elizabethan structure, and a block projecting north along the east wing. The different periods of masonry can best be seen in the medieval gatehouse and the splendid inner porch of c.1600.

Location	Nr Cowbridge, Vale of Glamorgan
Map ref	ST 009721
Tel	01443 336000
Web	www.cadw.wales.gov.uk
Open	Access at reasonable times

Pembroke

Pembroke began as an oval earthwork enclosure builtin the 1090s by Roger de Montgomery on a rocky promontory by the river. It grew into one of the grandest of the earlier castles in Wales with stonework added during the 12th and 13th centuries by William Marshal, one of King John's staunchest allies.

A massive great tower

Pembroke's dominating feature was, and still is, its cylindrical great tower built *c*.1200–10 by Marshal. It is a massive, four-storey structure rising from a splayed plinth to almost 24.5m (80ft) with thick walls and capped by a remarkable stone dome. The castle's enclosure was divided into two, an inner smaller bailey of triangular plan, two sides of which were cliffs overlooking the River Pembroke. The third side was a substantial curtain wall with flanking towers (a trapezoid-shaped stone hall was built in this bailey in the 12th century) and the larger outer bailey. This was enclosed with a stone curtain and several cylindrical corner towers on the angles, a twin rectangular-towered gatehouse and a powerful postern tower. Part of the southern curtain wall along the outer bailey was of double thickness for extra defence.

History

Pembroke escaped attack by Owain Glyn Dwr in the 15th century, but the castle was severely slighted after the Civil War and the local people plundered it for stone. For centuries it languished as an ivy-covered ruin, and it wasn't until the 19th century that the restoration of this great castle began. Henry Tudor, later King Henry VII, was born here in 1457.

In summer the castle stages historical re-enactments there are audio-visual exhibitions.

Location	Pembrokeshire
Map ref	SM 982016
Tel	01646 681510
Web	www.pembrokecastle.co.uk
Open	Daily 10–5 Mar & Oct; 9.30–6 Apr–Sep; 10–4 Nov–Feb

Picton

Amotte castle was built here *c*.1087–1100 at the top of rising ground. About 150 years later a second castle was raised near the original site. The new castle was a quadrangular enclosure with strong corner towers and mid-wall towers. The castle is still a home, and its last major remodelling was in the 1750s.

Visitor attractions

The property is sumptuously furnished and there are extensive woodland gardens. In the courtyard the gallery houses exhibitions. A restaurant is open for visitors.

Location	Haverfordwest, Pembrokeshire
Map ref	SN 011135
Tel	01437 751326
Web	www.pictoncastle.co.uk
Open	Castle & Gardens Tue–Sun 10.30–5. Entrance to castle by guided tour only (12–4)

Powis

Powis is a graceful residence of towers and battlements, mullioned windows and turrets incorporated into the site of a 13th-century castle. The original castle was destroyed by Llywelyn the Last in the 1270s because its Welsh owner sided with the English. It had two baileys, with a twin-towered gatehouse.

In the 16th century Powis came into the hands of Sir Edward Herbert, in whose family it remained until late in the 20th century. During the 16th century and again after the Civil War the buildings underwent extensive restoration and remodelling.

World famous gardens

Further work was carried out in all of the following centuries and Powis today houses an extensive collection of items from India in the Clive Museum, fine paintings and furniture. The world-famous garden has superb planting schemes, with Italian and French influences. Powis Castle has been under the care of The National Trust since 1952. There is a restaurant on site.

Location	Nr Welshpool, Powys
Map ref	SJ 216064
Tel	01938 551929
Web	www.nationaltrust.org.uk
Open	Thu–Mon 1–5 May–early Sep; 1–4 late Mar to early Apr & early Sep–Oct. Garden, days as castle, 11–5.30/6

Raglan

Raglan Castle may stand on the site of a Norman motte-and-bailey castle of *c.*1070. In the late 12th century, Raglan was granted to the Bloet family and a manorial complex, including a lord's hall, chapel and other domestic buildings was developed.

The Yellow Tower of Gwent

In 1432, it became the property of Sir William ap Thomas, a Welsh knight who had fought at Agincourt, and he started the structure whose magnificent ruins still dominate the landscape. His first building was a hexagonal-plan great tower, known as the Yellow Tower of Gwent. It was built *c.*1435–45, and stood surrounded by its own wide and deep ditch.

When the castle was enlarged by William Herbert *c.*1460–69, a great gate was built and an approach into the newer parts was created in the form of a three-storey forebuilding. The main gatehouse and the huge adjoining Closet Tower had gunports at parapet level. Ranging round two courtyards and with lavish domestic accommodation and polygonal towers, the castle became a fortress-palace.

The Civil War

In the early 16th century, Raglan Castle passed to Charles Somerset, who became the 1st Earl of Worcester. Succeeding earls transformed the castle into a great Tudor house with stunning gardens. The 5th earl sided with Charles I in the Civil War and Raglan was besieged from June to August 1646. It sustained a devastating bombardment for several weeks before surrendering. The castle was slighted and the Somersets used Raglan as a quarry for their new home at Badminton in Gloucestershire.

For visitors

Interpretative displays help explain the castle and this substantial ruin is a joy to visit.

Location	Monmouthshire
Map ref	SO 415083
Tel	01291 690228
Web	www.cadw.wales.gov.uk
Open	Daily 9.30–5 Apr–May & Oct; 9.30–6 Jun–Sep; Mon–Sat 9.30–4, Sun 11–4 Nov–Mar

Rhuddlan

A motte-and-bailey castle was raised here in 1073: the mound can still be seen south of the second of Edward I's great fortifications in North Wales, built between 1277–86 under the supervision of Master James of St George.

History

This later concentric castle has a lozenge-shaped inner stone enclosure with towers at the north and south corners and substantial gatehouses at the east and west corners. Most of the polygonal outer curtain, which had flanking rectilinear turrets on every angle and occasionally mid-wall, was surrounded by a wide moat, the rest by the River Clwyd.

Four kinds of stone were used in the construction of Rhuddlan Castle: purple sandstone from a quarry near St Asaph, a red sandstone from Cheshire, yellow sandstone from Flint and a local grey limestone. The river was diverted to create a deep-water channel running for 3km (2 miles) from the sea and this 'canal' meant that building materials could be brought from many sources by ship.

Rhuddlan served as a civil administration centre. In the Civil War, it surrendered to Parliament in 1646; it was later slighted.

Location	Denbighshire
Map ref	SJ 024779
Tel	01745 590777
Web	www.cadw.wales.gov.uk
Open	Daily 10–5 Apr–Sep

St Fagans

A small castle of two enclosures, little remains of the original works, as they have been obscured by the 16th-century mansion built on the site.

Attractions for visitors

The superb Museum of Welsh Life in the parkland surrounding the castle includes over 40 buildings from across Wales, re-erected here. There are many activities and events which provide visitors with an insight into the language and culture of Wales. The castle itself is a magnificent manor house with tapestries and dark wood furniture while its grounds offer an important guide to gardening through the centuries. There is also a restaurant.

Location	Cardiff
Map ref	ST 120771
Tel	029 2057 3500
Web	www.nmgw.ac.uk
Open	Museum of Welsh Life daily 10–5

Skenfrith

Skenfrith is a quadrilateral enclosure with corner cylindrical towers, surrounding a round great tower with a semi-cylindrical buttress on its western side. The 13th-century tower had three floors. The first-floor entrance was reached by an external staircase. A trap-door gave access to ground level and a spiral stair in the buttress led to the second floor.

Location	Monmouthshire
Map ref	SO 457202
Tel	01443 336000
Web	www.cadw.wales.gov.uk
Open	Access at reasonable times

White Castle

Originally called Llantilio Castle and then named White Castle because of its masonry coating of white plaster, this was predominantly a defensive structure with little attempt to make it very generous as a residence.

An impressive stronghold

This castle, together with Skenfrith and Grosmont, was built to protect one of the main routes between England and South Wales. While the others were rebuilt when they came under the control of Hubert de Burgh in the early 13th century, White Castle, the first of the three to have been rebuilt in stone, was left unchanged, an impressive military stronghold. The central pear-shaped enclosure is flanked on the northwest and southeast by two outer enclosures, and all three are moated. The northern enclosure, or outer ward, has a 13th-century curtain wall with flanking cylindrical towers and an outer gateway; impressively, these outer defences are largely still intact.

The stone curtain of the central enclosure was erected c.1184–6, and at about the same time a square great tower was built. In the 13th century, the great tower was demolished

(its foundations are still visible), and flanking towers and a towered gatehouse were added to the existing curtain wall.

Later, various buildings were erected, including a hall, a solar and a kitchen and oven block. The castle's importance declined after the end of the Glyn Dwr campaign, and by the end of the 16th century it was becoming a ruin.

Visiting

Access to the outer ward is by a wooden bridge over the dry ditch and to the inner ward by a longer wooden bridge over the water-filled moat. Magnificent views and castle defences can be seen from the gatehouse.

Location	Llantilio-Crossenny, Monmouthshire
Map ref	SO 380168
Tel	01600 780380
Web	www.cadw.wales.gov.uk
Open	Wed–Sun 10–5 Apr–Sep; Mon–Tue (except Bank Holidays) Apr–Sep open and unstaffed; open access Oct–Mar

Ireland

THE MAJORITY OF IRELAND'S CASTLES WERE IMPOSED ON THE COUNTRY
BY INVADERS AND SETTLERS. THEY WERE PHYSICAL MANIFESTATIONS OF
IMPERIALIST DOMINATION AND AS SUCH WERE DEEPLY RESENTED, AND UNTIL
RECENTLY THEY WERE STILL SEEN AS SYMBOLS OF HATED FOREIGN RULE.

IN TOTAL, THERE ARE MORE THAN 3,000 CASTLES IN IRELAND. MOST ARE
OVERGROWN RUINS, BUT AN INCREASING NUMBER HAVE BEEN RESTORED
IN RECENT YEARS.

MANY CASTLE ENTHUSIASTS WILL SEEK OUT THE REMOTE AND FORGOTTEN
RUINS, AS OFTEN AS NOT FOR THEIR WONDERFUL RURAL SETTINGS AS FOR THEIR
HISTORY. BUT 'SET PIECE' CASTLES SUCH AS ENNISKILLEN, PARKE'S AND TRIM ARE
REMARKABLY PRESERVED AND LOVINGLY RESTORED AND ARE LIKELY
TO BE ON ANY LIST OF 'MUST-SEES'.

The castle at Adare, set beside the River Maigue, was among the biggest in Ireland. It began life as an earthwork enclosure with gateways, beyond which a ditch with additional banking was created. The Anglo-Normans added a timber palisade to the enclosure and, soon after, the first stone buildings.

First buildings

One was a rectangular two-floor hall on the edge of the river, outside the enclosure. The upper floor was the first great hall. This building has loops at ground level and, above that, remains of fine Romanesque round-headed windows in pairs. Inside the enclosure a rectangular-plan great tower with three floors was raised, about 13 x 12m (43 x 40ft). Today it is largely demolished, although one wall still stands to its original full height.

In the mid-13th century the palisade wall was replaced by a stone curtain with a gateway on the south side, which housed a drawbridge. Later, a second, larger hall building was erected, also with its south wall along the river edge. A major reconstruction in the 15th century added battlements, and the great hall took on its present form. Lord Dunraven completed more repairs in the late 19th century.

Visiting

New structural consolidation, conservation and repair mean that by 2007 the castle and grounds should be fully accessible. There is a restaurant in the heritage centre.

Location	Co. Limerick
Map ref	R 4746
Open	Guided tour only Jul, Aug and possibly Sep. Tours booked at Adare Heritage Centre (tel 061 396666)

Ardglass

Five separate fortified structures in Ardglass can be classified as castles, and they were all tower houses. The largest, Jordan's, has been restored and now accommodates a museum. It is rectangular, with two projections along the north wall, one of which had a spiral staircase up to the roof, serving the four storeys. The windows are narrow loops externally. Jordan's was built in the mid-16th century and is probably the oldest of the fortified buildings.

Visiting

After visiting Jordan's, which is on the seafront, explore the other tower houses, too.

Location	Co. Down
Map ref	J 5637
Tel	028 90 546552
Web	www.ehsni.gov.uk
Open	10–1 Tue, Fri & Sat, 2–6 Wed–Thu Jul–Aug

Askeaton

This is an oval enclosure of stone inside a larger enclosure that skirts a rock islet in the River Deel. It contains two rectangular buildings. One was begun as a large hall in the early 13th century by William de Burgo and was altered in the 15th century to form a tower house. A small tower to the west houses chambers and garderobes. The castle was slighted (purposely damaged) in the Civil War and is still in a ruinous state. Beyond the inner enclosure you can see the remains of a 15th-century banqueting hall, one of the finest medieval secular buildings in Ireland.

Location	Co. Limerick
Map ref	N 3450
Open	Open access

Athenry

Athenry Castle was linked to the town that expanded beside it during the Middle Ages, itself enclosed by a complex system of walls, towers and gates, much of which remains.

Development of the castle

In around 1235, Meiler de Bermingham founded a castle at Athenry on the River Clareen. It was surrounded by a roughly D-plan stone enclosure with round towers on the corners. Within a generation, Meiler's son, Piers, had raised the height of the first floor, lifting its ceiling and walls, and embellishing its entrance with the fine arched door at the southeast end. This was reached from outside by a staircase from the ground, probably of timber (a reproduction stair exists there today), and it was protected by a forebuilding.

At the same time Piers erected a banqueting hall. Among the decorations he inserted were unusual narrow windows with trefoil heads. In the 15th century, the tower was raised yet again to provide two more floors and the top of the tower was equipped with battlements. At this time, an entrance was added to the basement (previously it had been accessed by ladder) that was cut into the splayed plinth.

What to see

Inside the castle, which has been re-roofed, is an audio-visual presentation and exhibitions. The town itself is worth visiting too, for its fine walls and towers.

Location	Co. Galway
Map ref	M 5028
Tel	091 844797
Web	www.heritageireland.ie
Open	Daily 10–5 Apr–May, mid-Sep–Oct; daily 10–6 Jun–mid-Sep. Guided tours on request

Athlone

Athlone was one of the major fording points of the Shannon, recognized as such by Toirrdelbach Ua Conchobair (Turlough O Conor), King of Connacht and for a time *Ard Rí* (High King) of Ireland. In 1129 he raised a wooden castle adjacent to a bridge, which he had built across the river nine years earlier. This 'castle' was one of only seven recorded pre-Norman castles in Ireland.

Norman structures

After 1200 either Richard Tuit or Richard de Constentin may have replaced this early 'castle' with a motte and bailey style fortification but this was later burned. In 1210, King John ordered a stone castle here and renewed the wooden bridge. It seems that the old motte was encased in stonework and a new polygonal tower built upon it. This structure, albeit altered and modified, can be seen today.

Modifications and additions have been made, especially in the Napoleonic era, but some of the medieval curtain walls and relics of the D-plan towers remain. The castle was besieged several times most notably during the Confederate War of the 1640s and later during two dramatic sieges during the Williamite and Jacobite Uprisings of 1690–91.

Visiting

A visitor centre expands on the history of the castle and the town. Visitors enjoy colourful exhibitions and audio-visual presentations that make history come alive. The coffee shop will revive you after your visit.

Location	Co. Westmeath
Map ref	N 0341
Tel	090 6442100 / 6492912
Web	www.athlone.ie
Open	Daily 10–4.30 Easter/May–early Oct. Will open rest of year for groups by prior arrangement

Aughnanure

Sited on the edge of Lough Corrib, this is a substantial and particularly good example of an early 16th-century tower house, which today stands six floors high. The tower house was built by the O'Flaherty family upon the remains of a much earlier castle.

The buildings

The structure has square corner box machicolations on the external corners at third-floor level. The tower stands on a sloping plinth, rises to stepped battlements, and inside there are various gun ports, shot holes and fireplaces. On the first floor there is a fireplace with a flue going right to the top of the tower. Some of the ornamentation in the tower features, such as the windows and doors, is elaborate. You will see the remains of a banqueting hall in one of the outer courtyards.

Visiting the castle

Inside the tower house there are information panels on each floor and guided tours are available on request. The tower house has been carefully restored by the Office of Public Works, which now manages the property.

Location	Oughterard, Co. Galway
Map ref	M 1544
Tel	091 552214
Web	www.aughnanurecastle@opw.ie
Open	Daily 9.30–6 mid-Jun–Sep; Sat–Sun 9.30–6 mid-May to mid-Jun & Oct

Ballymote

This is an enclosure castle of the later 13th or very early 14th century. It is almost square with massive round towers on the corners, a D-plan flanking tower along east and west walls, and a sally-port or postern tower on the south wall. But its main structure is a huge gatehouse of two half-round towers of four floors flanking the entrance on the north wall. Ballymote's enclosing walls are – where they survive intact – over 3m (10ft). At some stage, the gatehouse towers were strengthened by the addition of a protective skin of outer walling.

The castle was erected by the de Burgo family, but was besieged and taken by the Ua Conchobair and MacDiarmaid families in the 14th century. Thereafter, Ballymote has a long history of further siege, capture, sale or lease.

Restored property

Ballymote appears to have been left unoccupied for long periods, although it has been restored. It is now a National Monument. However, if you want to see the interior, you need to get the key from the Enterprise Centre (071 9183992).

Location	Co. Sligo
Map ref	G 6615
Tel	071 916121
Open	Daily

WEAPONS

WEAPONS WERE ESSENTIAL EQUIPMENT IN MEDIEVAL TIMES. NOTIONS OF CHIVALRY DICTATED THAT SOME WEAPONS WERE MORE 'NOBLE' THAN OTHERS, WITH THE SWORD AT THE APEX, BUT BATTLE AXES, SPEARS, AND BOWS AND ARROWS WERE CENTRAL PARTS OF CASTLE ARMOURIES.

The nobility had swords that were beautifully made and which were often said to have special powers. The swords of ordinary soldiers were more modest, but even these were excellent examples of medieval technology. Light, flexible and razor-sharp, a sword could pierce armour and cut off limbs or heads with one blow.

Longbows were a speciality of England and Wales, and helped to change the nature of warfare in the 14th century. Usually made of yew, a longbow was as tall as the archer, with the arrows about half that length. Longbow archers had to be immensely strong, since pulling the bowstring back was very difficult. An idea of the force of these weapons can be gleaned from stories of them driving 10cm (4in) into solid oak. Archers trained on smaller bows when still boys, and their bodies developed strangely, with their arms and upper chests hugely muscled in comparison to their legs. A skilled longbowman could fire an arrow every 10 seconds if he was aiming carefully, but more than that if accuracy was not needed. In battle, a hail of arrows could devastate the enemy, as happened to the French army at the Battle of Agincourt.

Crossbows were less accurate but could fire farther. They required less skill to fire, but could take up to a minute to load, since their strings could not be pulled by hand, but had to be winched into place.

Artillery and gunpowder began to appear late in the 14th century. At first used in much the same way as trebuchets and mangonels, and firing stones as they did, early ordnance could strike fear into the hearts of castle defenders. These weapons did not rely on accuracy: they battered away at castle walls until they collapsed under their own weight.

Fortifications changed as a result of the developing sophistication and power of artillery. Tall castle walls were easy targets, and by the 16th century lower walls, often protected by thick earthen ramparts, were common. By then, traditional castles were much less needed for defence anyway.

The majority of castles were last used in conflict during the Civil War, but some, like Dover, continued in use until 1945, armed with the latest weapons.

Barryscourt

Barryscourt is a large tower house, which was built around the early 1500s by the Barry family who had a residence in the Carrigtwohill area from the 12th century. The first and second floors have been restored and refitted with replica period furniture. The ground floor houses an exhibition about architecture and the arts in Ireland from 1100 to 1600. There is a restaurant.

Location	Carrigtwohill, Co. Cork
Map ref	W 8273
Tel	021 4882218
Web	www.heritageireland.ie (charlesfort@opw.ie)
Open	Daily 10–6 Jun–Sep.

Bunratty

The castle and Bunratty Folk Park share the extensive grounds here and in a day you can see the restored castle and then stroll through a re-created 19th-century village.

Early history

Instigated by the Macconmaras and once the seat of the Thomond O'Briens, this is a vast great tower built in the mid-15th century. It has a rectangular central core with four massive square corner towers. Originally, it stood inside an extensive enclosure with various buildings, but these have almost disappeared. The rectangular core of the great tower is 19 x 12.5m (62 x 41ft) with walls over 2m (7ft) thick. These walls contain a number of mural stairs, straight and spiral. The northern wall, 3m (10ft) thick, contains the entrance, which leads straight into a great hall that is vaulted, as is the storage floor underneath.

Above the great hall is a second hall that was magnificently decorated with fine plasterwork in the 17th century and has now been restored. The core contains the only large rooms. The four huge corner towers, each five floors high and more than 7m (23ft) square, contain the many bedrooms, garderobes, a chapel, and a plethora of passages and stairways.

Visiting the castle

Opened to the public in 1960, it is Ireland's most complete and authentically restored castle. Visitors can see the range of rooms from the basement, through the kitchens and great hall to the chapel, bedrooms and private apartments of the earl and his family. The rooms are decorated with hangings, tapestries and wall panelling. Furniture dates from the 15th and 16th centuries and the rooms contain fine artefacts.

Visiting the folk park

Bunratty Folk Park, in the grounds and extending to 10.5ha (26 acres), includes more than 30 buildings in a living village that re-creates life in rural Ireland in the 19th century. Meet and chat with the Bean an Ti (woman of the house) and various characters including the policeman and schoolteacher, who give the site its character. Enjoy the tastes, scents, sights and sounds of this place as you stroll from house to house or around the delightful village complete with school, post office, doctor's house, hardware shop, printers and, of course, the pub. The folk park also has a tea house.

Location	Co. Clare
Map ref	R 4561
Tel	061 360788
Web	www.shannonheritage.com
Open	Daily 9–6.30 Jun–Aug; 9.30–5.30 Sep–May

Blarney

This is arguably Ireland's most well-known castle – although not everyone will realize that the Blarney Stone is housed in a castle.

The great tower

Blarney's tremendous rectangular great tower – one of the biggest in Ireland – has an interesting building history. It was erected in two stages. Firstly, in the early 15th century a small 6m (20ft) square turret, rising to four floors and containing small rooms, was built as part of some other construction that has since been superseded. This original turret, not then machicolated, remained as it was, until about 40 years later when the castle owner, Cormac MacCarthaigh, decided to restructure by imposing a huge rectangular great tower, 18.5 x 12m (60 x 39ft), with five floors, on the earlier building. He also incorporated the small square turret at its northwest corner, making the whole an L-plan tower. The new rectangle has walls around 3.5m (12ft) thick at the lower levels. The second floor of the rectangle is vaulted, and the tower has its own staircase in the north wall.

Blarney Stone

The most striking feature of the newer tower is the massive parapet with its machicolation all round the top of the fifth storey. On the top of the parapet are stepped battlements. In the 18th century the then owner added a Gothic-style extension at the south end; however, this was severely damaged by a fire in the 19th century. The castle is known for the Blarney Stone, set in the machicolation. By leaning back head down between two machicolations you can kiss the stone, an act that will, it is claimed, 'confer eloquence'. The origin of the word 'blarney' meaning to talk persuasively but without malice is thought to date from the 16th century. Cormac MacCarthaigh was ordered to give the castle to the Crown. Rather than refuse outright, he delayed the event by inventing a series of excuses. Queen Elizabeth is reputed to have referred to this as 'blarney'.

Other attractions

The keep is surrounded by a lake, gardens and an arboretum, and there are woodland and garden walks. Explore Rock Close with its druidic connections and an eerie atmosphere that is especially scary in the dark. Blarney House in the grounds dates from 1874 and is open for tours in the summer. Refreshments are available.

Location	Co. Cork
Map ref	W 6174
Tel	021 4385252
Web	www.blarneycastle.ie.
Open	Mon–Sat 9–6.30, Sun 9.30–5.30 May, Sep; Mon–Sat 9–7, Sun 9.30–5.30 Jun–Aug; Mon–Sat 9–dusk Sun 9.30–dusk Oct–Apr

Carrickfergus

This large three-ward castle (the wards are from differing dates) is on the northern shore of Lough Belfast. The first of its three building phases was carried out between 1178 and 1195 and begun by John de Courcy, the Anglo-Norman lord who conquered much of Ulster. This early phase included the polygonal enclosure (which remains) and is called the inner ward, together with a great hall along its east wall, now only in a fragmentary condition. The other work of this phase was the nearly square great tower that still dominates the castle and the adjoining town today.

English administration

The castle was taken over by King John in 1210 and he made it an administrative centre for the English government, which it remained for more than seven centuries. The second phase of building in 1216 included finishing the great tower and adding a middle ward. This was done by erecting a wall west to east ending in a square tower on the edge of the lough, and a further stretch of wall north to south

feeding into the inner ward's walling to the south. The third phase, in around 1226–42, consisted of an outer ward on the north with a twin cylindrical-towered gatehouse to the north. The towers were about 12m (40ft) in diameter and flanked a passage protected by a portcullis. On the first floor of the eastern of the two towers is a chapel.

During its turbulent life Carrickfergus has also served as a prison, armoury and air-raid shelter.

What to see

Carrickfergus, maintained by the Environment and Heritage Service, is a self-guiding establishment. Information boards around the castle allow you to explore at your own pace while learning about its history, although guided tours are also available. Life-size model historic figures exhibited around the castle bring its past to life. Most activities for visitors take place in the keep, from armour demonstrations and exhibits (in May) to medieval games. Lively demonstrations and exhibitions take place throughout the year.

Location	Carrickfergus, Co. Antrim
Map ref	J 4187
Tel	028 9335 1273
Web	www.ehsni.gov.uk/places/monuments/carrick.shtml
Open	Apr–May, Sep Mon–Sat 10–6, Sun 2–6; Jun–Aug Mon–Sat 10–6, Sun 12–6; Oct–Mar Mon–Sat 10-4, Sun 2-4

Carrick on Suir (Ormond)

This is a superb mansion that deserves to be visited. It has been restored to a high standard and houses armour and paintings and hangings. The state rooms are particularly interesting for their fine decorative plasterwork and oak panelling. There is a restaurant on site.

History

This Elizabethan undefended house and courtyard was built by the Earls of Ormond and attached to a double-towered stone enclosure castle of the mid-15th century. The towers, of slightly differing dimensions but nearly parallel, were both five-storeyed, and one wall of each continued southwards and parallel to a joining wall at right angles, forming a courtyard. This latter wall was removed in the 16th century. The Elizabethan house at the northern end is lower than the earlier towers and is two-storeyed with a steep, gabled attic storey and impressive porch.

Location	Co. Tipperary
Map ref	S 4021
Tel	051 640787
Web	www.heritageireland.ie
Open	Daily 9.30-6.30 mid-Jun to early Sep. Guided tour only

Cashel

Approaching Cashel from Urlingford you can see, some distance before reaching the town, the High Rock of Cashel, 30.5m (100ft) above the plain. This was where Cormac, a 4th-century king in Munster, built his capital.

Early history

In the next century St Patrick visited the stronghold and it became an important centre of Christianity. Several of the kings of Munster became bishops. Brian Boru, later to become *Ard Rí* (High King of Ireland) and the greatest figure in Irish history was crowned there in the 970s as Munster's king. A century after his death in 1014 at Clontarf, his descendants gave the land to the Church and in 1127 Cormac MacCarthaigh started to build the small Romanesque church known later as Cormac's chapel. In 1169, a cathedral was started next door, where in 1172 the assembled Irish clergy paid homage to Henry II.

By the 1260s the cathedral had gone, but it was replaced by another, the ruins of which remain. At the end of the nave of this later building, a tower house was built in the early 15th century, 12.5 x 9m (41 x 30ft) and some 22m (72ft) tall, with thick walls and lots of passages; this is also now a ruin.

Hall of the Vicars

It is, however, possible to visit the restored 15th-century Hall of the Vicars, complete with its minstrels' gallery. This is one of Ireland's most popular attractions with some lovely silverware among the exhibits.

Location	Co. Tipperary
Map ref	S 0741
Tel	062 61437
Web	www.english-heritage.org.uk
Open	Daily 9-5.30 mid-Mar to mid-Jun; 9-7.30 mid-Jun to mid-Sep; 9-4.30 mid-Sep to mid-Mar

Castle Ward

An early 17th-century tower house in good external condition stands in the grounds of the 18th-century mansion, which is now in the care of the National Trust. The tower is 8.5 x 8m (28 x 26ft) and rises 15m (49ft) to the stepped battlements. The estate stretches to 332ha (820 acres), with fabulous views of Strangford Lough.

For visitors

It is the curious Gothic and Classical façades – due to differing opinions about the style of the house between its owner and his wife – that will strike you first. The castle and estate include landscaped gardens with woodland walks, a wildlife centre, a fortified tower house, Victorian laundry, theatre and a working corn-mill. The Victorian Past Times Centre will appeal to children, who can dress in period clothes and play with toys from the 19th century and there is an adventure playground in the grounds. There is also a tea room. These days Castle Ward is also the setting for the annual outdoor summer Festival of Opera.

Location	Strangford, Downpatrick, Co. Down
Map ref	J 5250
Tel	028 4488 1204
Web	www.nationaltrust.org.uk
Open	House and wildlife centre daily 1–6 Jun–Aug, times vary rest of the year. Grounds daily 10–8 May–Sep; 10–4 Oct–Apr

Donegal

The market town itself makes a good base for exploring the Donegal Bay area. However, don't miss this well-renovated castle.

Building works

A great tower castle was started here in the late 15th century by the O'Donnell family, lords of Tyrconnel. It has been greatly altered, disguising its original form although not concealing its obvious defensiveness. The tower was set on fire by the O'Donnells in about 1600 to prevent it being captured by the Earl of Essex's successor, Mountjoy. Then, a few years later the castle came into the possession of the Brookes, a prominent Protestant family, who carried out several major reconstructions, adding a substantial residential three-floor rectangular wing on the great tower's west side. The tower itself was restored, windows were enlarged, and a huge bay window was inserted just above the original entrance on the east side.

Visiting the castle

Donegal has been renovated and is furnished throughout. Information panels chronicle the history of the castle's owners. Guided tours are available.

Location	Co. Donegal
Map ref	G 9377
Tel	074 97 22405
Web	www.heritageireland.ie
Open	Daily 10–6 mid-Mar–Oct; Fri–Sun 9.30–4.30 Nov–Mar

Dublin

Dublin is possibly the castle least liked by the Irish because it was the headquarters of English government for so many centuries. The castle has been through numerous changes, so that it is not possible today to get any real idea of what it looked like in the late Middle Ages. But there is much of interest to see today. The first works were at the start of the 13th century and they were positioned on or near fortifications that were almost certainly of mid-10th-century Viking origin.

Early features

A drawing of the late 17th century shows the castle as a five-sided enclosure, with no great tower, but with huge round corner towers on the angles. Parts of some of these have survived, incorporated in various later works. These include the base of the Bermingham Tower on the southwest end of the enclosure; parts of what is now the Record Tower, 17m (56ft) in diameter, on the southeast end, whose parapet and machicolation are of the 19th century; and stretches of the southern curtain. What was known as the Storehouse Tower, on the northeast corner, may have been used as a residential tower in place of a great tower, but it was demolished in the 18th century. On the northwest corner was the Corke Tower, a round tower, rebuilt in the 17th century.

What to see

You can spend a day seeing everything here. The Chester Beatty Library has a collection of exquisite manuscripts, early Bibles and Korans, Oriental clothes and samurai uniforms and other objects from Asia, the Middle East, Africa and Europe. The State Apartments, the Chapel Royal and Undercroft give a glimpse into the life of the castle as a venue for state occasions (the State Apartments are occasionally closed for this purpose) and its history. The castle can only be viewed on a guided tour. The Garda Museum, in the Record Tower sometimes opens in the summer.

Location	Co. Dublin
Map ref	O 1534
Tel	677 7129
Web	www.dublincastle.ie
Open	Castle Mon–Fri 10–4.45, Sat, Sun 2–4.45 May–Sep; Mon–Fri:10-4.45, Sat, Sun 2-4.45 Oct–Apr. Chester Beatty Library Tue–Fri 10–5, Sat 11–5, Sun 1–5

Dunguaire

This 16th-century castle is raised on an old Irish ring fort that stands on a rocky promontory in a commanding position on the shores of Galway Bay. It rises to four floors and an attic, and the lower part of one of its walls makes up part of the wall of a six-sided surrounding bawn, or defended courtyard. The castle takes its name from the nearby ancient fort of Guaire, King of Connaught who died in 662 A D.

A home for centuries

In 1924 Oliver St John Gogarty surgeon, poet, author and wit, a contemporary and friend of W B Yeats and Lady Gregory, bought the castle as a place of quiet retreat and undertook much renovation. Today, visitors get an insight into the lifestyles of the people who lived at Dunguaire from 1520 to modern times, and the site bridges 13 centuries of Irish history, from the skirmishes, battles and sieges that characterize its colourful past, through to the literary revival of the early 20th century.

Location	Kinvara, Co. Galway
Map ref	M 3811
Tel	091 637108
Web	www.shannonheritage.com
Open	Daily 9.30–5.30 May–Oct. Banquet nightly 5.30, 8.45 Apr–Oct (reservations necessary)

Dunluce

One of the most dramatically sited castles in Ireland, Dunluce stands on a rock surrounded by the sea. It is attached to the mainland by a wooden bridge, formerly joined by a drawbridge. The castle was originally a four-sided enclosure, approximately rectangular, with corner towers. Of this oldest work only the south wall facing the land and the remains of two eastern towers survive. It had been erected on the site of a prehistoric souterrain, later a Christian 'underground' harbour for ships. The Norman castle buildings were begun by Richard de Burgo, Earl of Ulster. The main part of the castle is from a much later date, and includes a late 13th-century gatehouse. The great hall was erected against a somewhat earlier and rather unusual arcaded gallery, or *loggia*, and some of these pillars remain.

For visitors

An audio-visual presentation explains the history of the castle and brings it all to life. The castle's wonderful surroundings include a picnic area and the ruins of St Cuthbert's Church.

Location	Bushmills, Co. Antrim
Map ref	C 9041
Tel	028 2073 1938
Web	www.northantrim.com/dunluce
Open	Mon-Sat 10–6, Sun 2–6 Apr–Sep (Sun 12–6 Jul–Aug); Tue-Sat 10–4, Sun 2–4 Oct–Mar

Enniscorthy

A major Norman castle overlooked the Slaney River here in the 13th century, but it has mostly disappeared under a rebuild of the late 16th century and later modifications.

The plan may have been the same as at present, a rectangular, four-floor tower (with a cross-wall) with four cylindrical towers clamped on the corners. The two corner towers on the west wall act as protector towers for the main tower entrance. In the 16th century the castle was given to the poet Edmund Spenser by Queen Elizabeth I in recognition of his poem *The Faerie Queen*, dedicated to her.

A role as a museum

The castle now houses the tourist information office in the summer and it also acts as a museum, the County Wexford Historical and Folk Museum,

Permanent displays include an old Irish farm kitchen, early modes of travel, nautical memorabilia, and items connected with Wexford's role in Ireland's struggle for independence, especially the 1798 and 1916 risings.

The collections are varied and some items date to the Stone Age.

Location	Co. Wexford
Map ref	S 9739
Tel	054 35926
Open	Mon–Sat 10–8, Sun 2–8 Jul–end Aug

Enniskillen

Enniskillen Castle was at the centre of Irish rebellion against English rule in the 16th century. In 1508 it was besieged by both O'Donnell and O'Neill, and though destroyed it was rebuilt.

Sir Hugh Maguire didn't oppose settlers, and was content under English rule. However, when Scottish settlers from neighbouring counties began to invade Fermanagh, Hugh turned to the English for help. When no assistance was forthcoming Hugh fought back, so starting the Nine Years War. In 1594, Enniskillen Castle was captured by Captain John Dowdall and withstood a terrific onslaught for eight days. The planters won the castle and the Maguires spent years trying to take it back until it was finally brought to ruin in 1602.

A new life

In 1607 Captain William Cole was appointed Constable of the Royal Fort at Enniskillen. Cole was responsible for building a fort on the site of Enniskillen Castle, adding the Watergate in about 1615–20.

Visiting the castle

As well as a full schedule of special exhibitions held throughout the year, Enniskillen Castle also shows award-winning displays and audio-visual displays about Fermanagh's archaeology, history and wildlife. The museum also offers a wide range of educational programmes.

Location	Co. Fermanagh
Map ref	H 2144
Tel	County Museum 28 66 325000; Inniskillings Museum 66 323142
Web	www.enniskillencastle.co.uk
Open	Mon & Sat 2–5, Tue–Fri 10–5 May–Sep; Sun 2–5 Jul–Aug; Mon 2–5, Tue–Fri 10–5 Oct–Apr

Kanturk

An early 17th-century castle built with a four-floor rectangular core. The windows take up much of the walls – unusual for a stronghouse which was originally intended to be defensible. It is said that the owner stopped work on the castle because neighbouring lords complained to the English Privy Council about the size and fortifications.

The castle, also known as The Old Court, is south of Kanturk town. Legend surrounds the reasons why the keep combines a variety of architectural styles. The National Trust handed the property to the Irish people in 2000.

Location	Co. Cork
Map ref	W 3801
Tel	021 4273251 (Cork Kerry Tourism)
Open	Open access

Kilkenny

At first a motte castle of *c*.1171, built by Strongbow and destroyed, presumably by the native Irish, in 1174, the castle in this important early Norman town was begun again by William Marshal during his years in Ireland (1207–12). The castle came into the possession of the Butlers, Earls (and later, Dukes) of Ormonde in the 15th century and, over the centuries, they carried out extensive remodelling of the original works.

Today, Kilkenny is a national monument and houses the Butler Art Gallery in the former servants' quarters. The castle itself reflects the work of the 19th century when the Long Gallery was built to hold the family's collection of portraits. The Drawing Room, Ante Room, Library and Chinese bedroom are all open to visitors. Outside, the grounds include a rose garden, extensive woodland and a playground. In summer a tea room is open.

Location	Kilkenny
Map ref	S 5155
Tel	056 77 21540
Web	www.kilkenny.ie/hist/castle.html
Open	Daily 10.30–5 Apr–May; 9.30–7 Jun–Aug; 10.30–6.30 Sep; 10.30–12.45, 2–5 Oct–Mar. Last tour 1 hour before closing. Check before visiting for unscheduled closures in winter

Limerick (King John's)

Overlooking the River Shannon, the first building here was started in about 1200, on the site of an Anglo-Norman earthwork enclosure of six sides, which were rapidly converted to stonework.

Building works

The early building may have included a large round tower at each end of the west wall, a twin round-towered gatehouse in the northern wall, and slightly to the northeast another large flanking tower. The gatehouse was, for a time, the residence of the castle's constable. In Edward I's reign (1272–1307) more building was carried out, including the start of work on a substantial great hall along the Shannon.

Limerick Castle was intended as an administrative centre to control not only the activities of the Irish northwest of the Shannon but also to check the expansionism of Norman lords. It has been altered over the centuries because of its key role. It was captured by Edward Bruce in 1316, and was briefly in the hands of the O'Briens in the mid-14th century. It subsequently declined in importance and was re-occupied in the 17th century. A British army barracks was built in the courtyard in c.1750.

Major excavations began at the castle in the early 1990s. The most interesting result has been the exposure of significant remains of the 13th-century great hall, built in two stages.

What you will see

The castle, in the medieval district on King's Island, presents its long history to visitors through various media including animation and interactive effects, multi-media shows, exhibitions and excavated pre-Norman houses and fortifications. The remains of a medieval garrison and soldiers' quarters were more recently discovered, and the archaeological excavations are open to the public.

Location	Co. Limerick
Map ref	R 5857
Tel	061 360788
Open	Daily 9.30–5.30 Apr–May; 9–6 Jun–Aug; 9.30–5.30 Sep–Oct

Malahide

Although this much-modernized castle was the home of the Norman family of Talbot for several centuries, the remains of the original castle have been almost completely obscured. Nonetheless the present structure is handsome, and may even be described as formidable-looking. It gives a good account of the Talbot family who lived in the castle from 1185 until 1973, save for a brief occupation by a follower of Cromwell lasting about 11 years. Henry II granted the lands of the last Viking ruler of Dublin to Robert Talbot, one of his Norman knights who had come over to Ireland with him in the 1170s.

There are some remains at ground and cellar levels, and the cylindrical tower on the eastern side is probably part of the first major rebuilding of the 16th century.

Visitor attractions

A major feature of Malahide Castle is the extensive collection of Irish portrait paintings, mainly from the National Gallery, which together with the beautiful Talbot Gardens, extending to almost 8ha (20 acres), attract visitors from around the world.

The Fry Model Railway in the grounds of the castle has handmade model Irish trains spanning the earliest days of rail transport to the present. Trains run through a miniature version of Dublin.

There is a restaurant on the site.

Location	Co. Dublin
Map ref	O 2446
Tel	01 846 2184
Web	www.malahidecastle.com
Open	Mon–Sat 10–5 Jan–Dec; Sun 10–6 Apr–Sep; Sun 11–5 Oct–Mar. Closed for tours 12.45–2. Fry Model Railway: Mon–Thu, Sat 10–5, Sun 2–6 Apr–Sep

Maynooth

Maynooth has a substantial great tower, one of the largest of its kind in Ireland, inside an enclosure that is roughly rectangular. Very close to the great tower's southeast corner is a large, three-floor gatehouse, and to the east of this is another rectangular tower, also rising to three floors. The great tower is an impressive ruin and rises over 21.5m (70ft).

A succession of owners

There is evidence of at least three stages of building of the great tower, from the first work of *c*.1200 up to the 15th century. Building was probably begun by the Offaly Fitzgeralds. In the 1530s the castle belonged to 'Silken Thomas', Lord Offaly, who was the son of the Lord Deputy, Gearoid Og, the 9th Earl of Kildare. In the 'Thomas' rising of 1534–5 Thomas declared himself an enemy of the king who had arrested the 9th Earl and removed him to the Tower of London. The uprising was over when Maynooth, thought to be unassailable, was taken by the new Lord Deputy, William Skeffington. Those in the castle were killed and Thomas and his uncles were taken to London where they were executed as traitors.

Maynooth was returned to the Offaly Fitzgeralds in 1552, and was finally abandoned halfway through the 17th century.

Restoration

Maynooth was acquired by the state in 1991 and restoration began in 2000 and is ongoing. There is an exhibition on the history of the castle and the family, and there are guided tours of the keep, plus a restaurant.

Location	Co. Kildare
Map ref	N 9337
Tel	01 628 6744
Open	Mon–Fri 10–6, Sat– Sun 1–6 Jun–Sep

Parke's

This lovingly restored early 17th-century plantation castle, in the form of a tower house with extensions, is a formidable building.

Early life

Parke's started as a 16th-century rectangular tower house, with both east and west walls much thicker than the other two. Around it was a five-sided bawn with round flanking towers on two corners (north and northeast) of differing sizes. Part of the bawn, which seems to be of later date than the original tower house, skirts the edge of Lough Gill. There are traces of other buildings along the inside walls.

After the defeat of the Spanish Armada in 1588, the English destroyed the tower house, allegedly because its owner had given sanctuary to a sea captain, Francisco de Cuellar, who later described his stay when recounting his adventures. Stone from the tower was used in the 1620s by Robert Parke to build a plantation castle inside the bawn, using the east bawn wall as one of the sides and rebuilding the round flanking tower as part of his new tower house. The old tower was levelled.

Extensive work has restored the castle and the buildings that open to the courtyard, including a smithy. There are audio-visual exhibitions and guided tours.

Location	Fivemilebourne, Leitrim
Map ref	G 7835
Tel	071 916 4149
Web	www.heritageireland.com
Open	Daily 10–6 mid-Mar–Oct

Portumna

This is a substantial stronghouse-type mansion of c.1610–18 built by Richard Burke (de Burgos), 4th Earl of Clanricarde, Lord President of Connacht, who it is believed did not see his palace completed. Above the door there is box machicolation at parapet level. The four corner towers clamped on to the central rectangular core represented a formidable all-round defence by means of battlements and more gun ports. Most rooms were of massive proportions, and some surviving fireplaces are huge. The fortress-residence stands in its own bawn with strong round turrets at the east and west ends of the northern wall, with gun-ports along the east and west bawn walls. The castle was gutted by fire in 1826.

New life

Restoration began in the 1970s and conservation is ongoing. The grounds, too, have been subject to extensive renovation, including restoration of the 17th-century walled kitchen garden, now re-planted with fruit, vegetables, herbs and trees. The ground floor is open and there are guided tours and exhibitions in the castle and the gatehouse.

Location	Co. Galway
Map ref	M 8502
Tel	090 9741658
Web	Email portumnacastle@opw.ie
Open	Open daily 10–6 Apr–Oct

ROYAL CASTLES

THE STORY OF THE CASTLES OF BRITAIN AND IRELAND IS INEXTRICABLY LINKED WITH THE CHANGING FORTUNES OF KINGS AND QUEENS. AS MONARCHS CAME AND WENT, SO CASTLES WERE BUILT, DESTROYED AND REBUILT, ACCORDING TO THE CIRCUMSTANCES OF THE TIME.

William the Conqueror depended on his barons, and on the castles they built, to impose Norman rule and to keep rebellion firmly under control.

As the centuries wound on, and society became more settled, castles were often used by monarchs as temporary headquarters when they toured the country. Their retinues often ran into hundreds of people – servants, advisers, soldiers, secretaries, tax collectors and the like. They all needed housing and feeding, so castles were not only bustling at such times, they were also at the heart of the local economy. Foodstuffs were required in huge quantities but also bedding material, clothing, and all of the other paraphernalia required by what amounted to a small travelling town.

The most famous royal castle is the Tower of London. Begun by William the Conqueror, it was added to and changed by successive monarchs. It was a royal residence for 500 years, and has served the monarchy in many ways – as storehouse, armoury, mint, treasure vault and prison. The Crown Jewels are still kept there.

Today's primary royal castle is Windsor. It is the oldest surviving continuously occupied castle in the world. William the Conqueror built it to guard the western approaches to London and much remains unchanged: the outer walls follow the same lines as those erected by William, and his great motte stands at the core of the castle. However, many monarchs have changed Windsor. St George's Chapel is one of its primary buildings – this was begun by Edward IV and completed by Henry VIII. No fewer than ten British monarchs are buried here.

George IV made many changes, both inside and out, transforming Windsor's exterior into a vision of Gothic perfection. Queen Victoria and Prince Albert spent much time here, and they opened parts of it to the public for the first time.

The great fire at Windsor Castle in 1992 damaged or destroyed a fifth of this great complex, but restoration was completed by 1997, allowing this most special of castles a new life in an age where the future of the monarchy itself is in more doubt than the future of castles.

Roscrea

The first evidence of building here is documented: King John had a motte castle erected in 1213, but nothing of that remains. Then in about 1280, a stone castle was built beside the earthwork. It was a rambling enclosure, vaguely polygonal in shape, with a substantial rectangular gatehouse inserted in the northernmost wall. The gatehouse rose to three floors (and higher still in the 17th-century work). At much the same time, a round tower was added at each end of the south part of the enclosure, which was chevron in plan. Later in the 15th century the gatehouse entrance was sealed to make a tower house, and entry to the castle was through a new gateway in the wall next to the converted building.

The castle was occupied by the Butler Ormonde family. Inside the enclosure there is a Queen Anne mansion, called Damer House, which was built in the early 18th century.

What you will see

Considerable restoration work has been undertaken both to the castle and the fine mansion, Damer House, which sits alongside the castle in Castle Street, and is managed by the Office of Public Works in conjunction with the Roscrea Heritage Society. The centuries-old blocked entrance to the original gatehouse has been opened up making it a gatehouse once again, and the drawbridge and portcullis have been re-created.

The castle is accessible for groups in off-season – telephone to arrange this. There are also guided tours and exhibitions.

A restored mill stands beside Roscrea's Round Tower, and opposite the 12th-century Romanesque gable of St Cronan's Church. The exhibition in the mill gives an insight into the history of the town's heritage. It includes the Roscrea Pillar Stone and St Cronan's Cross.

Location	Co. Tipperary
Map ref	S 1389
Tel	050 521850
Web	www.heritageireland.ie
Open	Daily 10–6 mid-Mar to Oct

Thoor Ballylee

This 16th-century four-floor tower house overlooking the Cloon River at Ballylee, near Gort, was built for the de Burgo family. Each floor contained one room, reached by a stone spiral staircase built into the thick outer wall. The stairs lead to the flat roof and battlements.

Home to W B Yeats

The castle was purchased in 1916 and converted into a home for the poet, William Butler Yeats. For 12 years he spent his summers in the castle, and he wrote most of his important work here. After Yeats left in 1929 it fell into disrepair, but it has been restored as a national monument to him.

Two thatched cottages stood beside the castle, but only one has survived. Attached to the castle, it now serves as an interpretative centre containing a collection of first editions of Yeats' work, items of furniture and an audio-visual exhibition devoted to the poet.

Views from the top of the castle include surrounding countryside and Coole Park, an extensive nature reserve.

Location	Ballylee, nr. Gort, Co. Galway
Map ref	M 4403
Tel	091 631436
Open	W B Yeats Museum: Mon–Sat 10–6 Jun–Sep

Trim

Trim is among the greatest of the Norman castles in Ireland. Built by Hugh de Lacy in 1173 beside the River Boyne, it occupies just over 1.5ha (4 acres) and has hardly been altered since the 13th century.

The building work

The site is dominated by a massive 32m (105ft) stone keep. The core walls are a minimum of 5.5m (18ft) thick, although the turrets are about half this. The tower on the north wall is missing today although fragments remain of where it was keyed into the core.

It is believed the stone keep was erected in three stages: the first, from around 1176–96, had two levels – a ground floor over a basement; the second, about 1196–1206, added another level; the final phase in 1206 added a fourth floor which was the new great hall.

Scars on the walls show the line of the original roof from 1176. The windows of the first stage were long and narrow and these were subsequently widened to allow more light to enter and to facilitate the attachment of wooden hoardings. The entrance to the keep is at the first-floor level. There was a wooden staircase in the east tower that was later protected by forebuildings added in the late 13th century and the east tower held a chapel above the donjon. The first floor of the early work was divided in two by a cross-wall, providing a public hall, and the lord's private apartments. When the core was heightened, the new floors contained a variety of rooms.

Excavations

When Trim was excavated in the 1970s, remnants of more buildings were uncovered. A ditch around the keep yielded finds from

the 13th century, including pottery and arrowheads. The castle was neglected in the second half of the 14th century, until 1399 when Richard II on his famous journey to Ireland, arranged for two of his Crown wards to be imprisoned there. They were Henry of Monmouth (later Henry V) and his cousin Humphrey, son of the Earl of Gloucester.

Little is known of the great structure in the 15th and 16th centuries. It was finally yielded to Cromwell's forces in 1649, who fortified it until their departure in 1660. Work to prepare for visitor facilities in the 1990s has exposed the remains of medieval buildings

Visiting Trim Castle

Following conservation work, Trim Castle was opened to the public in 2000. Visitors have two options – they can access the keep by guided tour or they can explore the grounds of the castle where interpretative panels allow for self guiding. The conservation work won the Office of Public Works (the Irish State Body responsible for National Monuments) the Europa Nostra Award (an EU cultural heritage award) in 2003.

Scenes from the 1995 epic movie *Braveheart* were filmed here.

Location	Co. Meath
Map ref	N 8056
Tel	041 98 80300
Web	www.heritageireland.ie.
Open	Daily 10–5 Apr–Sep; daily 10–5.30 Oct; 10–5 Nov–Mar. Sat and Sun 10-5. Last admission and guided tour 1 hour before closing. If you wish to visit the keep you should arrive as early as possible

Glossary

adulterine unlicensed castle

apse circular or polygonal end of a tower or chapel

arcading rows of arches supported on columns

arrow-loop or slit long, narrow (usually vertical) opening in wall or battlements. Round or triangular ends were for cross-bows, as were horizontal cross-slits which gave greater range

ashlar blocks of smooth, squared stone of any kind

bailey or ward courtyard within the castle walls

barbican outward defensive continuation of a gateway or entrance

barmkin, bawn yard surrounded by outer defensive walling

barrel vault semicircular roof (stone or timber)

bartizan small turret projecting from the corner or flank of a tower or wall, usually at the top

bastion tower or turret projecting from a wall or at the junction of two walls

battlements or crenellation the parapet of a tower or wall with indentations or openings (**embrasures** or **crenelles**) alternating with solid projections (**merlons**)

belfry tall moveable tower on wheels used in sieges

buttress projecting pillar added to strengthen a wall

corbel stone bracket projecting from a wall or corner

cross-wall internal dividing wall in a great tower

curtain general word for walling enclosing a courtyard. Sited between towers, or tower and gatehouse, and appearing to hang between them

donjon alternative name for a great tower

drawbridge wooden bridge (which could be raised and lowered) across a ditch or moat

dressing carved or smooth stonework around openings and along edges

forebuilding structure on the outside wall of a great tower protecting the entrance and all or part of the approaching stairs. Some forebuildings contained chambers and chapels over the stairs

gallery long narrow passage or room

garderobe latrine

gatehouse room over the castle entrance

great tower or keep the main tower of a castle

gun loop or gun port opening in a wall for a gun

hoarding defensive covered wooden gallery placed above a tower or curtain. Floor was slatted to allow defenders to drop missiles or liquids on to besiegers

jamb straight side of a doorway, archway or window

light windowpane or window division

lintel horizontal beam of wood or stone positioned across the top of an opening

machiolation projecting part of a stone or brick parapet with holes in the floor, as in hoarding

mangonel stone-throwing machine

meurtrière or murder hole opening in the roof or a gateway or part of gatehouse over an entrance. Popularly believed to be used in the same way as hoardings, but might have enabled defenders to channel water to wooden areas set on fire by attackers

motte a mound on which a castle was built (man-made or natural)

oriel window projecting curved or polygonal window

oubliette dungeon or pit reached by trap-door used for holding prisoners (in Scotland a pit prison)

palisade a defensive fence

pele tower small tower house

pilaster buttress buttress with a projection, positioned in corner or mid-wall

pipe rolls accounts prepared annually by sheriffs for the king

plantation castle castles built in Ireland on land given to those who would support the Crown

portcullis wood and iron grille-pattern gate, raised and lowered in grooves at an entrance

postern small gateway, usually at the side or rear of a castle

quatrefoil four-lobed, six-foil six-lobed; trefoil three-lobed

quoin dressed corner stone at an angle of a building

relieving arch arch built in a wall to relieve the thrust on another opening

revet face with a layer of stone for more strength. Some earth mottes were revetted with stone

rib vaulting arched roof with ribs of raised moulding at the groins (junction of two curved surfaces)

rubble uncut or only roughly shaped stone, for walling

scarp inner wall or slope of a ditch or moat (counterscarp: outer wall or slope)

slight to damage or destroy a castle to render it unfit for use

solar lord's parlour or private quarters

stepped recessed in a series of ledges

stronghouse a mansion capable of being defended

turret small tower

wall-walk path along the top of a wall protected by a parapet

wing wall wall descending the slope of a motte

yett iron gates protecting an entrance

Index

Useful Addresses

ENGLAND
English Heritage
Customer Services,
PO Box 569, Swindon
SN2 2YP
Customer services
tel 0870 333 1181
Membership enquiries
tel 0870 333 1182
www.english-heritage.org.uk
Details of the regional offices are given on the website

The National Trust
36 Queen Anne's Gate,
London SW1H 9AS
tel 0870 609 5380
www.nationaltrust.org.uk
Details of the regional offices are given on the website

SCOTLAND
Historic Scotland
Longmore House, Salisbury Place,
Edinburgh EH9 1SH

tel 0131 668 8600
www.historic-scotland.gov.uk

The National Trust Office for Scotland
Wemyss House,
28 Charlotte Square,
Edinburgh EH2 4ET
tel 0131 243 9300
www.nts.org.uk

WALES
The National Trust Office for Wales
Trinity Square, Llandudno
LL30 2DE
tel 01492 860123

Cadw
Plas Carew,
Unit 5/7 Cefn Coed,
Parc Nantgarw,
Cardiff
CF15 7QQ
tel 01443 336000
www.cadw.wales.gov.uk

IRELAND
The National Trust Office for Northern Ireland
Rowallane House, Saintfield
Ballynahinch, Co. Down
BT24 7LH
tel 028 9751 0721

Environment and Heritage Service Northern Ireland
Historic Monuments Enquiries,
Waterman House,
5-33 Hill Street,
Belfast, Co. Antrim
BT1 2LA
tel 028 9054 3037
www.ehsni.gov.uk

Office of Public Works (Ireland)
51 St. Stephen's Green,
Dublin 2,
Ireland
tel 00-353-1-6476000
LoCall 00353 1890 213414
www.opw.ie

Acknowledgments

The publishers would like to thank all the castle owners and custodians who generously provided pictures and checked the information contained in this book, as well as the following people for their involvement: David Lyons for his numerous pictures, Bill Zajac at Cadw, and Antoinette Robinson at the Office of Public Works, Marilynne Lanng for research and editorial work, Laura Gil Lasheras for additional research, Pamela Stagg for proofreading, and Lisa Wyman for page design.

Disclaimer

The information in this book was correct at the time of going to press. However, the information is intended to be used as a guide only and readers are advised that they should contact the individual castles to check the information is correct prior to visiting. The publisher can accept no responsibility for inaccuracy and any inconvenience caused.